033450108

W9-BIT-240

DISCARD

Florida

Florida

Ann Heinrichs

Children's Press®
A Division of Grolier Publishing
New York   London   Hong Kong   Sydney
Danbury, Connecticut

Frontispiece: A young girl feeds the seagulls.

Front cover: Sanibel Island

Back cover: An orange grove

Consultant: Carole Fiore, Youth Services Consultant, State Library of Florida

Please note: All statistics are as up-to-date as possible at the time of publication.

Visit Children's Press on the Internet at http://publishing.grolier.com

Book production by Editorial Directions, Inc.

Library of Congress Cataloging-in-Publication Data

Heinrichs, Ann.
    Florida / Ann Heinrichs.
      p. cm. — (America the beautiful. Second series)
    Includes bibliographical references (p.) and index.
    Summary : A brief introduction to the geography, history, natural resources, indus-
tries, cities, and people of Florida.
    ISBN 0-516-20632-X
    1. Florida—Juvenile literature. [1. Florida.] I. Title. II. Series.
F311.3.H45 1998
975.9—dc21
                                           97-40706
                                             CIP
                                             AC

Acknowledgments

I wish to thank innumerable employees of the Florida Department of State's Division of Historical Resources for their kind assistance in this project. I am also grateful to Dick and Joyce Bizot of Jacksonville for their insights and to Steve Dobson of Englewood for his art.

Gulf Islands National Seashore

Seabirds

The space shuttle

An early rocket

Contents

Tampa skyline

Walt Disney World

Orange packing

Bottle-nosed
dolphin

CHAPTER ONE

Sun and Fun—Is There Room for Everyone?

Billy McCabe used to trot his cattle right down Bear Creek Road. On either side, goldenrod bloomed as far as he could see. Far across the rolling fields, wood storks drifted down to their nests by the pond.

Now 500 homes are going up in Billy's neck of the woods. A retail superstore just opened, and strip malls are coming soon. Muddy water from building sites floods the pond, and cars and bulldozers clutter the view. Traffic lights dangle over Bear Creek Road, and Billy is not sure how to get his cows to pasture anymore.

Here in Florida's rustic north, life is changing fast. Many families, like Billy's, settled here before the Civil War. Now their land is prime property for land developers.

Land booms are nothing new in Florida. Settlers snatched up land for plantations and orange groves. Once the railroads came through, resorts sprang up along the palm-lined coast. By the 1920s, even swampland was up for sale. Theme parks, recreation sites, and housing developments ate up land in later years.

Florida—nicknamed the Sunshine State—is one of the most popular places on the planet. Its endless beaches and sunny skies lure people from all over the world. In the 1980s, an average of 900 people moved to Florida every day!

A grove of cypress trees in Florida swampland

**Opposite:
South Miami Beach**

ALABAMA

Albany

GEORGIA

Alabama

Escambia

Dothan

Choctawhatchee

Lake Seminole

Oconee

Ocmulgee

Altamaha

Flint

Ochlockonee

Alapaha

St. Marys

ATLANTIC
OCEAN

Mobile

Ferry Pass

Pensacola

Apalachicola

Tallahassee

Suwannee

Jacksonville

Panama City

Apalachee Bay

Cape San Blas

Gainesville

St. Augustine

St. Johns

GULF OF
MEXICO

Lake George

Ocala

Ormond Beach
Daytona Beach
Port Orange

Deltona

Sanford

Titusville

Spring Hill

Altamonte Springs
Pine Hills
Orlando

Kissimmee

Merritt Island

Melbourne

N

Palm Harbor
Clearwater
Largo
Pinellas Park
St. Petersburg

Lakeland

Brandon

Tampa

Winter Haven

Palm Bay

Peace

Kissimmee

Fort Pierce
Port St. Lucie

0   50   100 mi.

0   50   100 km

Bradenton

Sarasota

Port Charlotte

BRIGHTON
SEMINOLE
RESERVATION

*Lake
Okeechobee*

West Palm
Beach

Caloosahatchee

Cape Coral

Fort
Myers

BIG CYPRESS
SEMINOLE
RESERVATION

Sanibel I.

MICCOSUKEE
RESERVATION

Fort
Lauderdale
Hollywood

Hialeah

Miami

FLORIDA

- City
- ⊛ State capital
- ▢ Indian reservation

*The
Everglades*

Biscayne Bay

Cape Sable

Key
Largo

Florida Bay

Key West

Florida Keys

For every person who lives in Florida, four more people visit every year. Some come to play—at Walt Disney World or Miami Beach. Others come to explore—in shadowy swamps full of alligators and herons. And no one's trip is complete without tasting a fresh-picked orange or a slice of Key lime pie. That's the good news.

The bad news is that Florida's beauty and popularity can backfire. New homes and recreation areas are eating away at Florida's natural environment. This affects natives such as Billy, who have never been to a theme park or even to the beach. But it can also discourage visitors and new residents.

Sunshine State officials are determined to win the good news/bad news war to make sure Florida keeps growing and to preserve its natural wealth.

Crowds of people along Jacksonville's Riverwalk

Opposite: Geopolitical map of Florida

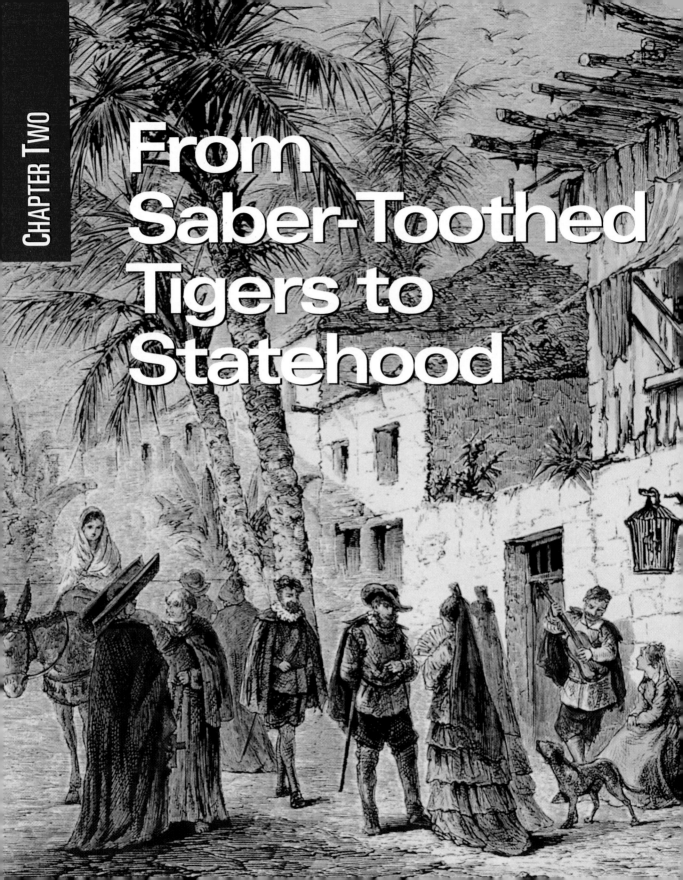

CHAPTER TWO

From Saber-Toothed Tigers to Statehood

Mastodons were among the prehistoric animals that lived in Florida.

People began settling in Florida as early as 12,000 years ago. The great Ice Age was ending, but much of today's ocean water was still frozen in polar ice caps, so the sea level was lower than it is today. Florida's land area was more than twice its present size.

On the opposite corner of North America, now-hidden land was also exposed. The Bering Land Bridge, where Alaska's Bering Strait is now, connected Asia and North America. People from Siberia crossed over in pursuit of big game animals. In time, their descendants made their way to Florida.

Mastodons, mammoths, camels, saber-toothed tigers, and giant armadillos roamed Florida's prehistoric grasslands. Prehistoric ancestors of today's turtles, manatees, sharks, and whales swam in the warm seawater.

Some early Florida residents were hunters who moved from place to place for fresh hunting grounds. They chipped stone to make spear points, arrowheads, and knives. From bones and deer antlers, they made fishhooks, needles, and other pointed tools.

Opposite: An early scene of St. Augustine

From Saber-Toothed Tigers to Statehood **13**

Fishing and Farming Cultures

By around 5000 B.C., people were settling along Florida's coasts and riverbanks. They lived on fish and shellfish and piled the bones and shells in huge middens, or trash heaps. Small animals, nuts, fruit, roots, and herbs rounded out their diet.

They used seashells as chopping tools and shaped tree trunks into canoes and wooden stakes. They wove clothes, baskets, and bags. For jewelry, they made beads and pendants of stone, bone, shells, and sharks' teeth. Their clay bowls, pots, and jars were painted with decorative patterns.

By around 1000 B.C., people were moving inland and settling into farming communities. They raised corn, beans, and squash and preserved extra food in storehouses. Their villages and ceremonial sites show that they had complex societies. Some groups carried on trade with people in present-day Georgia and Alabama. Burial mounds reveal that they buried pottery with their dead.

Florida first appeared on a Spanish map in 1502. At that time, about 100,000 American Indians lived in Florida. On the southern coasts were people of the Tequesta and Calusa cultures. The Ais lived along the central Atlantic coast. Timucuans occupied the central and northeast regions. The Tocobaga lived near Tampa Bay, and the Apalachee farmed and hunted in the northwest.

European Adventurers

Delicious rumors were floating around Spain in the 1500s. The New World across the Atlantic was laced with gold. And that wasn't all. Somewhere over there, the land was bubbling with

Crystal River Mounds

On the Gulf Coast near Crystal River is a 14-acre (5.7-ha) Indian ceremonial center. Prehistoric Indians used the site for eighteen centuries. People of the Deptford Culture (500 B.C. to A.D. 300) brought their dead there for burial. They were followed by the Weedon Island Culture (A.D. 300 to 1300). Today, visitors to the Crystal River State Archaeological Site can view the insides of burial, ceremonial, and midden mounds. ■

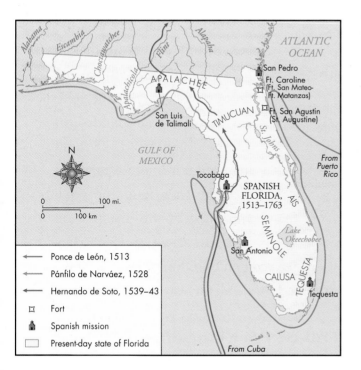

Juan Ponce de León

Juan Ponce de León (1460–1521), a Spanish explorer, was the first European to set foot on the North American continent. He sailed to the New World with Christopher Columbus in 1493 and was governor of Puerto Rico from 1509 to 1512. In 1513, he reached the Florida coast and founded the Spanish colony of *La Florida*. In 1521, he was killed by Indians during his second Florida expedition in search of the fabled Fountain of Youth. ▨

waters from a magical spring. Whoever drank from that spring would be young forever.

Juan Ponce de León was determined to find this Fountain of Youth. He was already in his fifties—quite an old man for the 1500s. He set sail and spotted Florida on March 27, 1513. A week later, he landed north of present-day St. Augustine. Because it was Easter time (*Pascua Florida* in Spanish), he named the place *La Florida.* But even a Fountain of Youth would not have saved Ponce de León from his fate. On a return trip in 1521, he was killed in an Indian attack.

Above left:
Exploration of Florida

Hernando de Soto

Hernando de Soto (1496?–1542), a Spanish explorer, was appointed Spanish envoy to Florida. He landed at what is now Charlotte Harbor in 1539. Looking for treasure, he trekked through the Florida swamps and continued through much of the southern United States. ■

Pánfilo de Narváez was the next Spaniard to try his luck in Florida. Narváez, still in his thirties, was going for the gold. He and his men landed in Tampa Bay in 1528 and marched north into Apalachee country. They found no gold, and most of the group were later lost at sea. In 1539, Hernando de Soto began his own expedition from Tampa Bay. His four-year march took him through Florida all the way to Oklahoma.

The Rise and Fall of Fort Caroline

Meanwhile, in France, a group of French Protestants called Huguenots needed refuge from persecution. Their leader, Jean Ribaut, sailed with René Goulaine de Laudonnière to a spot at the

De Soto National Memorial Park

Hernando de Soto's expedition included not only 600 men and women, but also horses, pigs, and other provisions. Historians believe they landed at the mouth of the Manatee River on Tampa Bay. That spot in present-day Bradenton is now a national memorial park. Exhibits trace de Soto's expedition and its importance in American history. Costumed rangers demonstrate the settlers' blacksmithing, cooking, and weaponry skills. ■

The Place of Slaughters

Two national monuments—Fort Caroline and Fort Matanzas—share a sad place in Florida's history. In 1564, 300 French Huguenots settled Fort Caroline, but Spaniards destroyed it a year later. Today Fort Caroline stands on the St. Johns River near Jacksonville. It has been rebuilt from drawings by Jacques Le Moyne, an artist among the French settlers.

Many of the French settlers escaped the massacre, but Spaniards caught them later along the beach south of St. Augustine and killed them. They named the spot *Matanzas* (Place of Slaughters).

In 1742, the Spaniards erected a watchtower at Matanzas as a lookout for British ships. It was built of coquina, a white limestone made of seashells and coral. The tower still stands on the 300-acre (121-ha) Fort Matanzas site. ■

mouth of the St. Johns River in 1562. They returned with a shipload of settlers in 1564 and built Fort Caroline—the first Protestant colony in the New World.

When King Philip II of Spain heard about the French colony, he sent Admiral Pedro Menéndez de Avilés to rout them out. In 1565, Menéndez de Avilés sailed into a natural harbor near Ponce de León's landing site. He set up a fort there and named it *San Augustin* (St. Augustine). This fort became the first European settlement in the New World that still exists today.

From St. Augustine, Menéndez de Avilés marched north and wiped out Fort Caroline. The Spaniards promised mercy but slaughtered almost all the Frenchmen and took over the French fort, renaming it San Mateo.

Life among the Timucuans

Around Fort Caroline, Timucuan Indians lived in circular villages surrounded by palisades, or protective fenceposts. They were organized into kinship clans but had no central leader. Their homes were cone-shaped, with roofs of thatched palm branches and walls of woven vines. They lived on shellfish from the St. Johns River and wild game from the forest.

Jean Ribaut described them as "naked and of goodly stature . . . very gentle, courteous and of a good nature." The men stood more than 6 feet (180 cm) tall. They tied their black hair in a top-knot, while women let their hair hang freely. Men wore animal skins and women wore Spanish moss. Tattoos were a mark of distinction. Chiefs encircled their mouths with blue tattoos.

At the time the French arrived, there were tens of thousands of Timucuans in the region. They had lived in northeast Florida for about 1,000 years. They gradually died off from diseases brought by the Europeans and from warfare with Spaniards and other Indian groups. By 1698, only about 550 Timucuan people were still alive. None are left today. ■

Spanish Florida

The Spanish colony soon stretched west to the Gulf of Mexico and north into present-day Georgia and South Carolina. Spanish governors ruled this vast colony from their capital at St. Augustine.

Franciscan missionaries came from Spain to convert the Indians to Christianity. They built about 140 missions, extending northward into Georgia and westward to Apalachee territory. One of the largest was San Luis de Talimali, near Tallahassee.

Doubling as military forts, the missions served the Spaniards more than they did the Indians. For the Indians, conversion went hand in hand with forced labor and military service. After a Timucuan Indian revolt in 1656, the Spaniards reorganized the mission system. But by the early 1700s, British and Indian raids had burned most of the Spanish mission-forts.

The British Rule—For a While

In 1763, European powers met to settle their Seven Years' War. As part of the bargain, Spain gave up Florida to Great Britain. Up went the British flag. East Florida and West Florida became the fourteenth and fifteenth British colonies in the Americas. St. Augustine was named the eastern capital, and Pensacola governed the west. West Florida now reached all the way to the Mississippi River and north to present-day Jackson, Mississippi.

Land grants lured settlers to the new colonies. Sugar, cotton, and indigo plantations sprang up along the St. Johns River. Cattle ranches and citrus groves prospered, and lumbering thrived.

The American Revolution (1775–1783) brought a fresh wave of settlers. Loyal British subjects from Georgia and South Carolina

Kingsley Plantation

Kingsley Plantation stands on Fort George Island at the mouth of the St. Johns River. From 1817 to 1839, it was Zephaniah Kingsley's sugarcane and cotton plantation. Kingsley, a territorial legislator, was married to a black woman. He believed that slavery could work if the slaves were treated kindly.

The main house and the remains of twenty-three slave cabins are still standing there. The site is Florida's oldest remaining plantation and part of Florida's Black Heritage Trail. ■

William Duval, the first governor of the Territory of Florida

moved south to find a safe haven in Florida. But British Florida lasted only twenty years. In 1783, Spain regained control of the colony.

The Territory of Florida

In the Adams-Onís treaty of 1819, Spain agreed to hand Florida over to the United States. On July 21, the Spanish flag came down at last. In 1822, President James Monroe signed a law establishing the Territory of Florida. East Florida and West Florida had now became one. William Duval became the first governor of the new combined territory.

Present-day Tallahassee was named the capital city in 1824. It was a compromise between westerners, who wanted Pensacola as the capital, and easterners, who favored St. Augustine. Lawmaking power rested in the hands of a legislative council of only thirteen people. They called their first meeting to order in a log cabin near the site of today's state capitol.

The Seminole Wars

For new settlers in Florida, the Seminole Indians were a nuisance. They took up valuable farmland and harbored runaway slaves. The U.S. government offered to resettle the Indians in Oklahoma. But under their courageous leader, Osceola, the Seminoles stood their ground. Soon, battles raged between the Indians and the U.S. army.

General Andrew Jackson subdued the Seminoles around the Suwannee River in the First Seminole War (1817–1818). The Second Seminole War dragged on for seven years. It began in 1835, when Seminoles ambushed Major Francis Dade, leaving only one survivor. Osceola was captured in 1837, but

Seminole Indians, led by Osceola, attack Fort King in 1835.

Osceola

Osceola Nickanochee (1804?–1838) was a great leader of Florida's Seminole Indians. He was born in Georgia, the son of a white pioneer and an Indian woman. In Florida, he led the Seminoles in battles against Andrew Jackson and in attacks on white settlers. These attacks led to the Second Seminole War. Osceola was taken prisoner during peace talks in 1837 and died in an army prison in South Carolina. ■

David Levy Yulee

David Levy Yulee (1811–1886) was one of Florida's first two U.S. senators. Yulee had worked hard to gain statehood for Florida. He served in the Senate from 1845 to 1851 and from 1855 to 1861. Coming from a Portuguese Jewish family, Yulee was the first Jewish member of the Senate. In the 1860s, he founded Florida's first railroad that crossed from the Atlantic to the Gulf. Both Levy County and the town of Yulee are named in his honor. ■

his people kept up the fight until 1842. Then hundreds of Seminoles were forced to move to Oklahoma.

Chief Billy Bowlegs led the Indians in a hodgepodge of swamp fights called the Third Seminole War (1855–1858). By the time it was over, most of the Seminoles had been wiped out. Only a few hundred survived by hiding out in the Everglades.

Statehood

By 1840, more than 54,000 people lived in Florida. Almost half the population were slaves who worked the territory's prosperous plantations. Many Floridians were pushing for statehood, but others were against the idea. They wanted to wait until the population was high enough to make two states. That way, a larger number of proslavery states would be represented in Congress. Others wanted Florida to remain a territory. Then the federal government would keep paying the territory's expenses.

Congress was divided over Florida statehood, too. As a southern state, Florida would add to the proslavery forces in Congress. The only way to keep the country at peace, it seemed, was to add one southern and one

Florida Joins the Union

In 1837, Floridians were asked to vote their wishes on the statehood issue. The results show how divided they were: 2,139 voted for statehood and 1,164 voted against it.

The U.S. Congress was split, too, as northerners and southerners fought to balance slave and free states. Florida applied for statehood in 1839 but had to wait six more years. Early in 1845, Congress passed the Florida statehood bill. President John Tyler signed it into law on March 3, 1845—his last day as president. Florida was now the nation's twenty-seventh state, although no one in Florida knew about it. It took five days for the news to reach Tallahassee!

As word got around, Tallahassee broke out in wild celebration. Citizens rang church bells, shot off cannons, and set bonfires. Territorial Governor John Branch held a lavish reception at Live Oak, the governor's mansion. ■

northern state at the same time. Finally, congressmen worked out a compromise. Florida would be admitted as a slave state and Iowa as a free state.

Florida joined the Union in 1845. William D. Moseley, a planter from Jefferson County, became the first state governor.

Historical map of Florida

From Saber-Toothed Tigers to Statehood **23**

CHAPTER THREE

War and Peace

n the 1850s, the slavery issue threatened to tear the country in two. While Florida was a slave state, only about one-third of the white households owned slaves. More typical was the lone homesteader in the wilderness. The wealthy planters had the most to lose if slavery were outlawed. They led the state in opposing the antislavery Republican Party.

Gamble Plantation, once a sugarcane plantation, served as a supply station during the Civil War. Today it is a state historic site.

When Republican Abraham Lincoln was elected president in 1860, feelings in the South exploded. South Carolina withdrew from the Union and formed the Confederate States of America. On January 10, 1861, Florida became the third state to secede. It joined the Confederacy a month later. In April, the Civil War began.

Florida Joins the Civil War

It's not surprising that Florida was split, even in wartime. About 15,000 Floridians signed up for the Confederate army, while more than 2,000 joined the Union forces. Florida's cattle supplied beef to the Confederate army. A special "cow cavalry"—the Cracker Cowhunters—protected the herds. Florida also furnished the Confederates with cotton, pork, fish, salt, and vegetables.

The Union navy blockaded much of the Florida coast, so that no ships could get in or out. Union forces held Fort Taylor in Key West, Fort Pickens in Pensacola, and Fort Jefferson in the Dry

Opposite: Packing oranges in the early 1900s

The Rise and Fall of a Plantation

Major Robert Gamble bought 3,500 acres (1,400 ha) of land near Bradenton in the 1840s. There, with the help of 200 slaves, he set up a sugarcane plantation and sugar refinery. Gamble built his ten-room house out of tabby plaster, a local building material made of crushed oyster shells and lime. When sugar prices dropped in the 1850s, Gamble had to sell his farm.

Confederate soldiers used the house as a supply station during the Civil War. After the war, the home was a hideout for Judah P. Benjamin. He had served as Confederate President Jefferson Davis's secretary of state. Benjamin eventually escaped to England. Today, Gamble Plantation is a state historic site. ■

Tortugas. Only a few battles took place in Florida, but Confederate soldiers scored heroic victories in two of them.

Florida's Confederates in Action

In 1864, Union forces marched deep into Florida. Their mission was to cut off Confederate supply lines, recruit black soldiers, and occupy Jacksonville. From there, they could take Tallahassee.

Confederate General Joseph Finegan knew the Union army was on the march. He positioned his troops at Olustee, between a lake and a swamp, with only a narrow passage between them. On

The capture of the gunboat *Columbine* along the St. Johns River in 1864

February 20, the two forces met and the battle began. On it raged until dark; Finegan was almost out of fresh troops. In the nick of time, the Union army retreated.

Confederates won another victory in the Battle of Natural Bridge. Union troops set out to destroy Confederates who had attacked them at Cedar Key and Fort Myers. They met at Natural Bridge near Tallahassee on March 6, 1865. The Union army battled all day long to take the bridge. But the Confederates defended it until the Union forces gave up and left.

Confederate General Joseph Finegan

Neither of these battles made a difference in the outcome of the war. It ended with a Union victory in April 1865. But Tallahassee had kept its freedom. It was the only Confederate state capital east of the Mississippi River that the Union army never controlled. On May 10, 1865, federal troops occupied Tallahassee at last.

Time to Rebuild

After the war, Florida's population was quite mixed. There were frontiersmen, freed slaves, Seminoles, and deserters from the army. Immigrants had arrived from Cuba, the Bahamas, Greece, and Italy. New settlers were given 160-acre (65-ha) parcels of land. A homesteader who lived on the land and cultivated it for five years would then own it.

Across the South, the federal government began its Reconstruction program. Federal troops occupied the Southern states, including Florida, and Republicans ran the state governments. These measures were meant to protect newly freed slaves and rebuild the war-torn economies.

Florida was readmitted to the Union when it abolished slavery in 1868. The old plantations were broken up among sharecroppers and tenant farmers. At the same time, northern investors poured fresh money into Florida's industries. By 1877, Florida's Democrats were back in control, and federal troops pulled out.

Growth and Prosperity

Florida saw a flurry of activity in the 1880s. Swamps were drained to make way for farms, citrus groves, and cattle ranches. Cubans in Key West and Tampa built a booming cigar-making industry. By 1890, Key West was the most populous city in the state. Greeks in Tarpon Springs dived for sponges off the coast. Phosphate, discovered near Tampa, soon became a major export.

Northern tourists began to notice Florida, too. Some enjoyed riverboat cruises, while others headed for seaside resorts. New railroad lines opened up the state for both

Henry Morrison Flagler

Henry Morrison Flagler (1830–1913) was a cofounder of the Standard Oil Company. In the 1880s, he settled in St. Augustine and built the Ponce de León Hotel (now Flagler College). In the 1890s, he built the Florida East Coast Railway (lined with more hotels) all the way down the coast to Miami. He continued the railway on bridges through the Florida Keys to Key West. From there, travelers on the popular train could ferry to Havana, Cuba. Flagler's Palm Beach mansion, Whitehall, is now a museum. ■

business and tourists. Henry Plant built railroads linking Jack-sonville to the Gulf coast. Thanks to the railroad, the seaport of Tampa became an important export center for Florida goods.

Boats in Key West

Henry M. Flagler's railroad reached Miami in 1896, and the city was incorporated that same year. Flagler made it easy for tourists to travel on his rail line. He built hotels all along the route. Before long, Flagler's own steamships were chugging from Miami to Key West and Havana, Cuba.

Frosty weather in 1894–1895 wiped out north Florida's citrus crops. Citrus growers moved farther south, clearing more land for settlement. By this time, they were growing both oranges and grapefruits.

During the Spanish-American War (1898), the United States agreed to help free Cuba from Spanish rule. After all, Florida and Cuba had enjoyed close ties for more than 300 years. U.S. troops camped in Miami, Tampa, and Jacksonville before heading off to Cuba. After the war, many soldiers settled in Florida with their families.

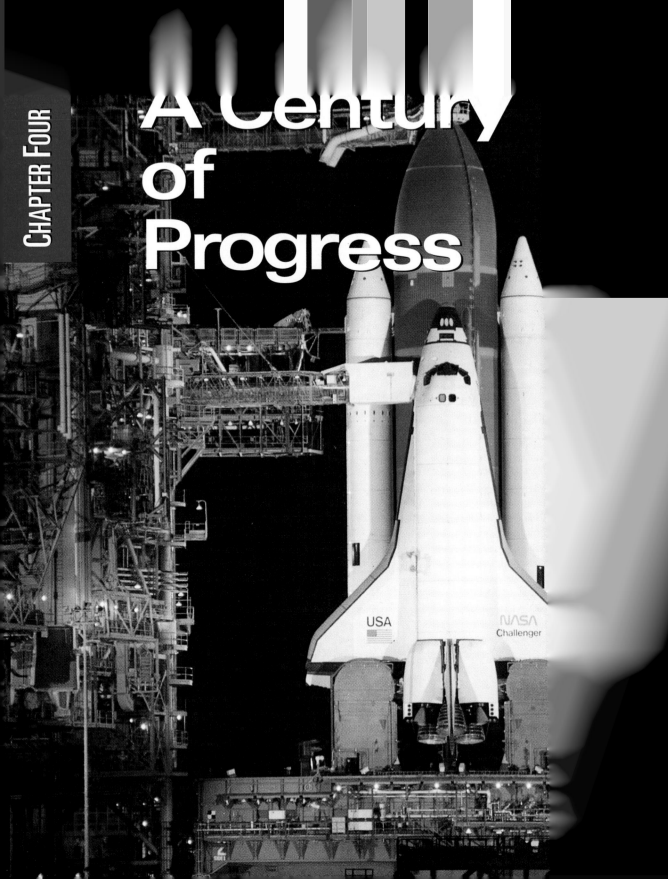

CHAPTER FOUR

A Century of Progress

Governor Napoleon B. Broward

The early 1900s were a golden age for Florida. Millionaires from northern states vacationed in Florida and built luxurious homes there. They brought their elegant lifestyles, fine arts, and recreations to the state. Hollywood producers fell in love with Jacksonville and made it a major movie-making town.

In 1906, Governor Napoleon Bonaparte Broward began a massive land-reclamation project. Canals were dug to drain Everglades swampland and make way for settlement. New communities spread westward from the heavily populated southern coast. With water from the canals, new residents had plentiful water supplies.

Land and housing sales boomed in the 1920s. More new cities sprang up, and more highways were built to reach them. Thanks to Henry Ford's new invention, tourists could now cruise down to Florida in their Model T automobiles. South Florida was especially popular. In a four-year span, the Miami area's population quadrupled.

Race Relations and Rosewood

In the years after World War I (1914–1918), violence against African-Americans swept across the United States. Mobs of whites raided black communities, burning homes and killing innocent people. The anti-black Ku Klux Klan was behind many of the raids.

Opposite: The space shuttle *Challenger* at Kennedy Space Center, Cape Canaveral

The Rosewood Incident

The violence in Rosewood began when a white woman said that a black man had come to her home and assaulted her. Eyewitnesses, however, reported that it was a white man who entered her home. Nevertheless, during the next few days, a mob of more than 200 white vigilantes burned Rosewood to the ground. Between eight and eighteen residents were shot. Others escaped into the freezing swamps and fled to nearby towns. Today, a few charred bricks are all that remains of Rosewood. ■

In Florida, 47 black citizens were lynched (executed by white mobs) between 1918 and 1927. The Rosewood Incident stands out as the worst event of that period. It occurred during the first week of January 1923, in the black township of Rosewood in Levy County.

From Bad to Worse

By 1926, land sales were out of hand. Prices rose to such insane levels that the whole market crashed. Banks failed, and wealthy people lost everything they had. To make matters worse, hurricanes in 1926 and 1928 wiped out much of south Florida.

With the stock market crash of 1929, the United States plunged into the Great Depression. That same year, Mediterranean fruit flies descended on Florida's citrus groves. About 60 percent of the crops were destroyed.

For Florida, the Depression era had a positive side. Land prices had dropped, so people from northern states moved in to snap up the bargains. Many of the newcomers built hotels and apartment buildings, which helped the state's economy. Floridians found low-cost ways to enjoy nature, too. The state park system opened in 1935 with nine parks.

The 1926 Miami hurricane destroyed homes and other property in south Florida.

Carl Fisher

Carl Fisher (1874–1939), an automobile magnate, built the Indianapolis Speedway in 1909. Turning to real estate, he helped change Miami Beach from a mangrove swamp to a popular resort. Fisher drained swampland, filled in the area with tons of sand, and sold land to wealthy buyers. To encourage tourists, he helped build the Dixie Highway from Chicago to Miami. ◼

Wartime and the Postwar Boom

During World War II (1939–1945), Miami, Daytona, and St. Petersburg were training centers for the U.S. Navy and Army Air Corps. Thousands of troops poured into Florida for training. Tourist beaches became staging grounds for military drills. Even the resorts joined the war effort. Tourist hotels became military quarters to house the troops.

After the war, many of the soldiers came back to Florida to settle down. By 1950, more than 2 million people lived in the state. Another 3 million visited as tourists every year, and a Florida invention—frozen concentrated citrus juice—had exploded into a major industry.

The U.S. Air Force began testing missiles at Cape Canaveral in 1950. In 1958, the National Aeronautics and Space Administration (NASA) launched *Explorer I* from Cape Canaveral. This was the first U.S. satellite to orbit the Earth. Five years later, after President John Kennedy was assassinated, the launch site was renamed Cape Kennedy.

A new era in Florida's history began in 1959. Fidel Castro's Communist revolution took over the island nation of Cuba. Cuban exiles poured into Florida, most of them settling in the Miami area. Through the next twenty years, more than 500,000 Cubans arrived as well as immigrants from Central and South America. Miami became known as the "Latin Capital of America."

Many Cubans came to Florida and made their own neighborhoods.

Space Highlights

1958 NASA begins operations at Cape Canaveral with the launch of *Explorer I*, its first Earth-orbiting satellite.

1962 John Glenn becomes the first U.S. astronaut to orbit the Earth.

1963 John F. Kennedy Space Center opens. Cape Canaveral is renamed Cape Kennedy by President Lyndon Johnson (later changed back to Cape Canaveral).

1969 *Apollo 11* astronaut Neil Armstrong becomes the first person to walk on the moon.

1971 In the *Apollo 15* moon mission, astronauts spend three days exploring the moon.

1973 Space station *Skylab* is sent into orbit.

1975 *Apollo 18* and Soviet *Soyuz* astronauts link their spacecraft together in space.

1981 The first space shuttle blasts off from Cape Canaveral.

1983 Sally Ride (right), aboard space shuttle *Challenger*, is the first American woman in space.

1986 *Challenger* explodes shortly after liftoff. All seven astronauts aboard are killed. NASA holds off on manned space-flights for almost three years.

1997 In NASA's *Pathfinder* mission, a computerized robot vehicle explores Mars.

1998 On Russia's space station *Mir*, U.S. astronauts begin spacewalks to assemble the International Space Station. ■

Modern Challenges

Development versus the environment—these two forces have been at war for most of the twentieth century. In the 1980s, the legislature began passing laws to protect Florida's natural resources. State lawmakers are determined to balance conservation with human needs.

Florida's cities, like others around the United States, are battling crime and illegal drugs. The drug trade has been one of Florida's worst problems. Florida is a prime spot for South American drug traffickers to bring drugs into the United States. And along with the drug trade comes crime.

State and federal law-enforcement officials have cracked down hard on drug trafficking in Florida, but crime continues to be a problem. In the mid-1990s, Florida ranked first in the nation in its rate of violent crimes.

Florida's ever-increasing immigrant population is another problem. With the collapse of the Soviet Union in 1991, Cuba lost its major source of aid and trade. This, plus a revolution in Haiti, brought a new surge of immigrants into Florida. The cost of providing education and health services for all of the new arrivals is overwhelming.

Florida took its place on the world stage in December 1994 when Miami hosted the Summit of the Americas. It was the largest gathering of world leaders ever assembled in the United States.

Attendees were the heads of 34 democratic countries in North, Central, and South America and the Caribbean. They agreed on ways to work together on industry, trade, human rights, and the

environment. Every issue related to Florida in some way—from democracy in Haiti to pollution control. For Florida, the meeting was a great way to join its international neighbors in building a vision of the future.

World leaders gather at the Summit of the Americas in December 1994.

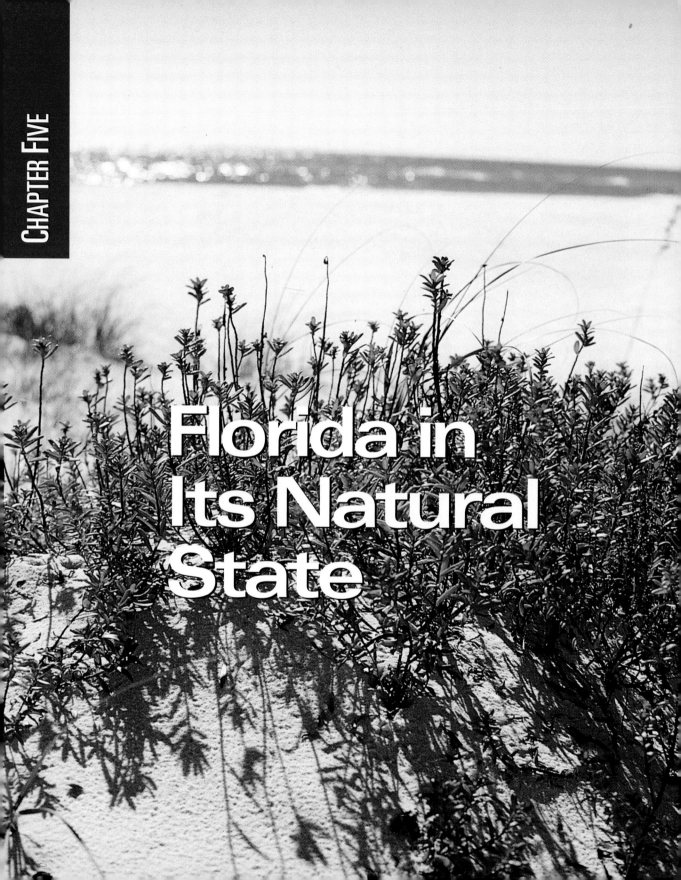

CHAPTER FIVE

Florida in Its Natural State

Florida was one of the last parts of North America to emerge from the sea. When dinosaurs thundered across the continent to the north, Florida was still under water. Layers of limestone gradually settled upon the bedrock until land appeared above the surface.

Florida's coral reefs are beautiful and fun to explore.

Fourteen states make up the region called the South, and Florida is the southernmost. The only state that lies farther south is Hawaii. Compared to other states, Florida is medium-size—twenty-one states are larger, and twenty-eight are smaller.

By land, Florida borders Georgia and Alabama. Its long, thin northwestern strip is called the Panhandle. The rest of the state is a peninsula, surrounded almost completely by water. In fact, no point in Florida is more than 60 miles (97 km) from the sea. Eastern Florida lies along the Atlantic Ocean, while the west coast and southern Panhandle face the Gulf of Mexico.

Coastal Lowlands

The powdery, white sand on the northern Gulf coast squeaks when you walk on it. That's because it's made of round-edged grains of quartz. Geologists say this sand washed down from the Appalachian Mountains thousands of years ago. On the Atlantic coast, the sand is made of shells and coral. Its rough-edged grains "pack" better, but they don't squeak.

Opposite: Gulf Islands National Seashore

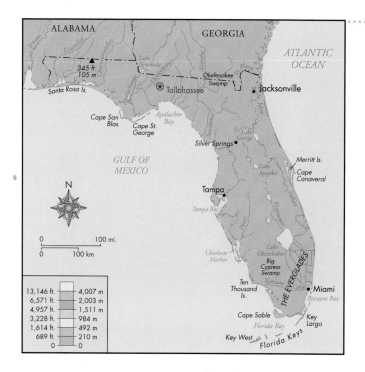

Florida's topography

Florida has the longest coastline of any state except Alaska. Most of Florida's big cities, industrial areas, and resorts were built along the coast. The famous sandy beaches are just one feature of Florida's coastal lowlands. Much of the east coast is lined with pine forests and windswept dunes. On the west coast, facing the Gulf of Mexico, are countless bays, inlets, and mangrove swamps.

Hundreds of sandbars, coral reefs, and islands are just offshore. Florida's barrier islands are narrow strips of land up to several miles long. They form a breakwater, sheltering the coast from pounding waves and violent storms.

The Everglades

The Everglades region covers the whole southern end of Florida's mainland. It is the largest swamp in the world. This "river of grass" looks like an endless, grassy meadow. But the grass actually grows from the bottom of the swamp's shallow waters. Parts of the Everglades region have been set aside as Everglades National Park and Big Cypress Swamp.

Inland Florida

Pine and hardwood forests cover the highlands of north Florida and the northern Panhandle. While this is higher ground than the

The River of Grass

Native Americans called the Everglades the "River of Grass." Its basin, often flooded, is a sawgrass prairie and swamp 40 miles (64 km) wide and several inches deep. Everglades National Park, the third-largest national park in the continental United States, covers 1.5 million acres (607,030 ha).

The massive wetland is a worldwide "celebrity" too. UNESCO (United Nations Educational, Scientific, and Cultural Organization) has named the Everglades a World Heritage Site and an International Biosphere Reserve.

Cars cross the Everglades on the Tamiami Trail (U.S. highway 41) or Alligator Alley (Interstate 75). For an up-close look, nature lovers hike along several popular trails. They encounter gnarled mangroves, sawgrass prairies, fern groves, and forests of mahogany and slash pine.

Birdwatchers in the Everglades track herons, egrets, flamingos, ibises, and spoonbills. Alligators (above), crocodiles, and turtles are common sights, as well as coral snakes, water moccasins, and diamondback rattlesnakes. The Everglades is the only place in the world where alligators and crocodiles live together naturally. ▪

Florida's Geographical Features

Total area; rank	59,988 sq. mi. (155,368 sq km); 22nd
Land; rank	53,997 sq. mi. (139,851 sq km); 26th
Water; rank	5,991 sq. mi. (15,517 sq km); 7th
Inland water; **rank**	4,683 sq. mi. (12,129 sq km); 4th
Coastal water; **rank**	1,308 sq. mi. (3,388 sq km); 6th
Geographic center	In Hernando County, 12 miles (19 km) northwest of Brooksville
Highest point	In Walton County, 345 feet (105 m)
Lowest point	Sea level along Atlantic Ocean
Largest city	Jacksonville
Longest river	St. Johns River, 275 miles (443 km)
Population; rank	13,003,362 (1990 census); 4th
Record high temperature	109°F (44°C) at Monticello on June 29, 1931
Record low temperature	– 2°F (–19°C) at Tallahassee on February 13, 1899
Average July temperature	81°F (27°C)
Average January temperature	59°F (15°C)
Average annual precipitation	54 inches (137 cm)

coastal areas, no place in Florida is really very high. The state's highest point—near Lakewood in the Panhandle—reaches only 345 feet (105 m). That's about twenty stories shorter than Miami's tallest skyscraper!

The north is also known for its springs and sinkholes. A sinkhole occurs when porous limestone beneath the topsoil gives way. The ground simply caves in. Hundreds of sinkholes happen every year, some opening up huge underground caverns. Florida's biggest known sinkhole is 320 feet (97 m) wide and 150 feet (46 m) deep. In 1981, when it caved in, it swallowed up six cars and a house!

From the Georgia border down to Lake Okeechobee are Florida's central highlands, which are partly hilly and partly flat. Vast prairies covered this region in prehistoric times, but it looks quite different now, with thick forests, ranches, farms, and citrus groves. Okefenokee Swamp, lying mostly in Georgia, spreads across the Georgia border into northern Florida.

The Keys

The Florida Keys curve like a tail from the mainland's southeast corner. (Their name comes from the Spanish word *cayo,* meaning "small island.") About 3,000 islands make up this 150-mile (241-km) chain. They are the fossilized remains of an ancient coral reef built on a limestone base. The offshore reef along the Keys is the only living coral reef in the continental United States and the only underwater state park.

The Florida Keys

People live on about thirty of the Keys. Key West, at the end of the line, is the southernmost point in the continental United States. It lies just 90 miles (145 km) from the Caribbean nation of Cuba.

Lakes, Rivers, and Springs

About one-twelfth of Florida's surface area is water. Some 30,000 lakes are scattered through central Florida. Many of them are broad, shallow ponds with grass growing up from the bottom. Lake Okeechobee is the largest lake in Florida and the second-largest freshwater lake completely within the United States. Only Lake Michigan is larger. Okeechobee is the middle link in a waterway that runs across the whole state from the Atlantic to the Gulf.

Pesky Plants

Strangler figs (above) are native Florida vines that wrap around a tree trunk, eventually killing the tree. Their usual victims are sabal palms.

Australian pines were introduced into Florida as shade trees, but they do more harm than good. Their thick foliage keeps other plants from growing under their branches.

Melaleucas, or punk trees, suck up water at an amazing rate. They were brought to the United States from Australia to help drain the Everglades but soon spread out of control. ■

Sawgrass growing among the hammocks

The St. Johns River is the state's longest river, flowing north to its mouth at Jacksonville. In Ocala National Forest, the river widens into Lake George. Rivers connect many of the lakes in Florida. One example is the Kissimmee River. Rising near Orlando, it threads its way through half a dozen lakes until it reaches Lake Okeechobee.

Rivers in the Panhandle rush southward to empty into the Gulf of Mexico. The largest is the Apalachicola, formed by the meeting of Georgia's Chattahoochee and Flint Rivers. The Suwannee arrives from Georgia, too. The Perdido River marks Florida's western border with Alabama.

Florida has more than 300 springs. Twenty-seven of them are classed as first-magnitude springs—they have an output of at least 64 million gallons (242 million l) a day.

Most of Florida's springs are in the north-central region. Some are gentle bubblers, while others are powerful gushers. Silver Springs, near Ocala, is the largest in the state. More than 500 million gallons (1,893 million l) of water gush from Silver Springs every day, making it one of the most powerful springs in the world.

Greenery Galore

Anyone hiking through a Florida forest is likely to come upon a hammock. Hammocks are "islands" of trees, often standing high

above the surrounding scrub. Holes in the soft limestone beneath them allow the roots to reach underground water.

In the forests that cover about half of Florida, pine trees are the most common species. Loblolly, slash, and longleaf pines grow in the uplands, while scrub pines grow on flat, sandy soil. In many areas, tall pine trees mix with ash, beech, sweet gum, hickory, and maple. Magnolias and stately live oaks are tropical hardwoods of the north. Growing in their shadows are flowering dogwoods and redbuds.

Palm trees give Florida its tropical look. Elegant royal palms line the city streets, while short, fan-leaved palmettos create underbrush in forests. Only fifteen types of palm are native to Florida, but hundreds of species flourish there. Coconut palms, sabal (cabbage) palms, and Washingtonia palms are among the common species.

Along the southern coasts stand mangrove trees, with their eerie, aboveground roots. Mangroves are the only trees in the world that can grow in salt water. Their roots help hold the shoreline in place and shelter hundreds of marine creatures. Cypress trees, on the other hand, can grow in fresh water. Some of the giant bald cypresses in Big Cypress and Corkscrew swamps are hundreds of years old.

Royal palms line the streets in Palm Beach.

Tough, sharp-bladed sawgrass forms the "river of grass" in the Everglades. It is one of the oldest plants in the world. Giant ferns grow in swamps and other moist soil, and Spanish moss hangs like long beards from the branches of old trees. This frizzy plant is an epiphyte—a plant that gets its nutrients from the air. Mistletoe, classed as a parasite, also grows in Florida.

Orchids, azaleas, and poinsettias grow wild in Florida. Florida wildflowers include gardenias, lilies, sunflowers, irises, and hibiscus.

Creatures of Land and Sea

Black bears, gray wolves, deer, wildcats, and foxes still roam the forests, as they have for hundreds of years. In the Everglades, only a few dozen Florida panthers survive. Some of Florida's smaller mammals are raccoons, squirrels, rabbits, skunks, and opossums.

The Key deer is a miniature species found only in the Florida Keys. This tiny, endangered deer stands 2 feet (60 cm) tall and weighs less than 75 pounds (34 kg). Speeding drivers kill about seventy of them every year.

Slinking through the swamps are six species of poisonous snakes, including the deadly water moccasins and rattlesnakes. Alligators and turtles dive for food or sun themselves on logs. As civilization pushes into the swamps, alligators pop up in surprising places. Trappers routinely remove the reptiles from swimming pools, schools, golf courses, and even hotel fountains.

Long-legged wading birds such as blue herons, egrets, and ibises thrive in the wetlands. Other native waterbirds are spoonbills,

The Key deer is found only in the Florida Keys.

wood storks, pelicans, and anhingas. Pileated woodpeckers, barred owls, gnatcatchers, mockingbirds, and cardinals flit through the woods. Many northern bird species, like humans, spend their winters in Florida. Others stop off in the wetlands before migrating farther south.

Manatees are gentle, slow-moving sea mammals that feed on water plants along the coast. Also called sea cows, they can grow up to 14 feet (4.3 m) long and weigh more than a ton. Manatees are endangered animals. About half of all manatee deaths are caused by humans—mostly by boat-propeller blades.

Bottle-nosed dolphins are another Florida sea mammal. These playful creatures live in the Gulf of Mexico. Intelligent and easily trained, they do lots of tricks in water shows. In the early 1990s, federal lawmakers prohibited feeding dolphins. They were afraid that the dolphins would begin to depend on humans and forget how to find their own food. However, this fear was unjustified, and the law was repealed after three years.

Bottle-nosed dolphins are playful animals.

Wonderful Weather

The Sunshine State is generally warm, sunny, and pleasant all year round. Surrounding waters cool off the peninsula in summer and warm it up in winter. Southern Florida's climate is tropical,

Floridians enjoy their state's warm climate.

with cycles of wet and dry weather. The north enjoys a temperate climate, much like that of neighboring southern states.

Florida winters are cool but rarely cold. Miami had its first recorded snowfall—just a light powdering—in 1977. Once in a while, though, an unexpected cold wave blows in. And if the temperature dips below freezing, Florida's precious citrus crops are in danger.

With about 54 inches (135 cm) of rainfall a year, Florida is the wettest state. Most of the rain falls during summer thunderstorms.

Hurricanes—Taking a Fearful Course

"Everywhere there was complete and total destruction . . . as the hurricane passed northward on its fearful course, leaving a graveyard of ships and lost souls." That's how a survivor described the hurricane that wrecked his fleet in 1733.

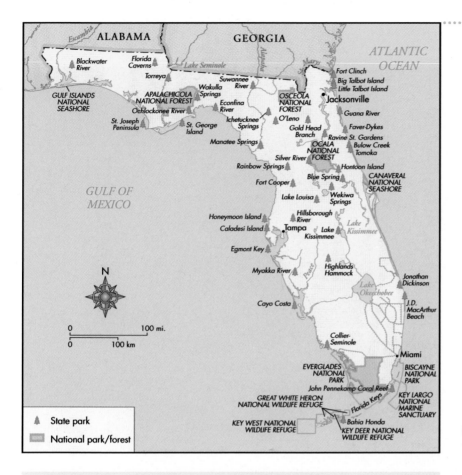

Florida's parks and forests

Conservation Issues

Logging and land development have been eating away at Florida's natural landscape. Once-abundant prairies have been replaced by farms and grazing land. Between 1940 and 1980, forestland decreased 27 percent; from 1982 to 1992, Florida's developed land grew by 35 percent. Since 1900, more than half the freshwater marshes in southwestern Florida have been drained.

Floridians have battled over the Everglades for almost 100 years. Some people want to use and develop the land, while others want to preserve it. Meanwhile, fertilizers and wastes from nearby communities are poisoning the waters and killing off many water and land animals. Florida's 1994 Everglades Forever Act aims to clean up the waters. ■

Merritt Island National Wildlife Refuge and Canaveral National Seashore

Just a couple of miles from here, space shuttles blast off on their space-age missions. But Merritt Island National Wildlife Refuge quietly preserves an ancient landscape. Its hammocks, or tree islands, have little forests that are hundreds of years old.

More than 500 animal species live in this refuge. Manatees, loggerhead sea turtles, alligators, armadillos, and bobcats are a few of the year-round residents. In winter, migrating birds from all over North America arrive here. More endangered species live on Merritt Island than in any other refuge in the Americas. Among them are bald eagles, with nests that measure 10 feet (3 m) across.

Along the east bank of Merritt Island is Canaveral National Seashore. There, sea turtles crawl ashore to lay their eggs on the sandy beach. A prominent landmark on the shore is Turtle Mound Archaeological Site, a 35-foot (11-m) mountain of oyster shells built up over many years. Spanish explorers could see it from far out in the sea. ■

In late summer, people living on the coast brace themselves for hurricanes. These violent tropical storms form in the Caribbean Sea and Atlantic Ocean. They gather speed as they race toward the coast, reaching wind speeds of up to 200 miles (322 km) per hour. Hurricanes strike as far north as New England and as far south as the Caribbean islands. "Hurricane Alley"—from Cape Canaveral to the Keys—gets the worst battering.

At least one hurricane hits Florida almost every year, but some years stand out as worse than others. The hurricane of 1926 leveled Miami. The 1935 hurricane killed 400 people on the Keys and the Gulf coast. In 1992, Hurricane Andrew devastated Dade County. Hurricane Opal wrecked the Panhandle coast in 1995. Today, the National Hurricane Center in Coral Gables warns residents when hurricanes are approaching on their "fearful course."

Hurricane Andrew

On August 24, 1992, Hurricane Andrew swept into southern Dade County in the most costly storm in Florida's history. It left 85 people dead, thousands injured, and 250,000 people homeless. The city of Homestead, south of Miami, was almost completely destroyed. ■

CHAPTER SIX

FIRST UNION

Florida Scenes, Old and New

Much of Florida looks just as it did a thousand years ago. Swamps, forests, reefs, and dunes are Florida's natural link to its prehistoric days. Alongside the old Florida is the new, human layer—farms, citrus groves, theme parks, and museums. A tour of the state, from the Panhandle to Key West, is a fascinating trip through both worlds.

The Panhandle

Much of the northern Panhandle is an unspoiled wilderness of pine forests and underbrush. In contrast, the southern Panhandle is a stretch of sparkling beaches with small towns, shrimp boats, and little seafood shacks. People wade along the shore looking for seashells and sand dollars.

In the far west, Gulf Islands National Seashore spills across the border into Alabama and Mississippi. The largest of the nation's ten national seashores, it includes six barrier islands. Its two historic forts—Fort Pickens and Fort Barrancas—fought each other during the Civil War.

Pensacola is the major city in the western Panhandle. Its three historic districts preserve the homes and belongings of early pioneers. East of Pensacola, small towns and miles of white-sand beaches line the coast.

Fort Walton Beach is the home of Eglin Air Force Base. Destin used to be a little fishing village, but its small-town days are

The wilderness of the northern Panhandle

Opposite: The Tampa skyline at dusk

Florida's cities and interstates

long gone. Today its beachfront is lined with luxury hotels and condominiums. Grayton Beach is still safe from the tourism boom. Its water and shoreline are clean, and boardwalks protect its dunes.

Panama City is overrun with college students during spring break and with northerners in the winter. Dolphin tours are the rage at Panama City Beach. Boats take people out into the Gulf, where they hop in to swim with the dolphins.

People in Apalachicola call their town Apalach for short. Their lumber mills closed down long ago, but their oystering tradition is still alive. Oystermen harvest the oyster beds in the bay, while their families sell handcrafts in the town's shops.

Tallahassee

History, nature, and modern state politics come together in Tallahassee, Florida's capital. The old, white-columned capitol and the new, 22-story capitol stand side by side. Nearby Park Avenue is lined with gracious mansions built in the 1800s. Throughout the city, ancient oaks and luxurious flowers preserve the flavor of the Old South.

A few blocks from the capitol is the Museum of Florida History. It covers 12,000 years of Florida's geology and history. Highlights include mastodon remains from nearby Wakulla Springs, a giant armadillo, and Spanish, British, and Civil War exhibits.

Native birds and animals roam the 52-acre (21-ha) wilderness behind Tallahassee Museum of History and Natural Science.

One of the many nineteenth-century mansions along Park Avenue in Tallahassee

Visitors might spot bald eagles, wolves, bobcats, or even a Florida panther. There is also a kids' discovery center and an 1880s farm, complete with farm animals.

Jacksonville

Jacksonville began as the town of Cowford, where herds of beef cattle crossed the St. Johns River. Today it's the state's largest city. As a shipping and manufacturing center, Jacksonville has a hard-working, blue-collar tradition. Its port is one of the busiest in the United States. The city is also home to three naval bases, including Jacksonville Naval Air Station.

Jacksonville Landing attracts both tourists and locals.

The St. Johns River winds through town, with Heckscher Drive along its north bank and a boardwalk on the south. Residents enjoy "hanging out" at Jacksonville Landing—a riverfront shopping, eating, and entertainment center.

Historic homes and gardens line the streets in the Riverside/Avondale Historic District. The Cummer Gallery of Art displays more than 2,000 works of art, dating from as early as 400 B.C. Other sites include historic Fort Caroline, the Museum of Science and History, and the Jacksonville Zoo.

Scattered at the mouth of the St. Johns River are the Sea Islands. Amelia Island, the largest, is steeped in history. Legendary pirates Blackbeard and Captain Kidd once lurked along its shores. Another Sea Island, Little Talbot, is a nature preserve. On nearby Fort George Island, visitors see traces of 5,000 years of human habitation.

St. Augustine

Historic sites throughout St. Augustine are reminders of its Spanish heritage. The old Spanish fort of Castillo de San Marcos over-looks Matanzas Bay. Completed in 1695, it is the oldest masonry fort in the United States. A moat and drawbridge once protected the fort, and costumed soldiers still fire its huge cannons.

Only foot traffic is allowed on cobblestone-paved St. George Street. This historic district includes the Spanish Quarter, a restored

Castillo de San Marcos in St. Augustine

Which Is the Oldest?

St. Augustine is famous as "the nation's oldest city." But that's the short version. More precisely, it's the oldest continuously inhabited *European* settlement in North America. Nearby Fort Caroline was founded a year earlier, but that settlement perished. The Hopi Indian town of Kykotsmovi, formerly Oraibi, in northern Arizona, is actually the oldest continuously inhabited settlement in the present-day United States. It dates from A.D. 1150. ■

Fort Mosé

Fort Mosé, north of St. Augustine, was America's first free black settlement. The African residents were runaway slaves from the Carolinas who were welcomed and protected by the Spaniards. They worked for pay in the St. Augustine community as soldiers, carpenters, and ranchers. The original fort was built in 1738 and rebuilt nearby in 1756. When Great Britain took Florida in 1763, the Africans moved to Cuba with the Spanish colonists. Fort Mosé became a National Historic Landmark in 1994. ■

village where people demonstrate the crafts and daily activities of the 1700s.

The oldest house in St. Augustine is now a museum on St. Francis Street. Its original Spanish walls were erected in 1727. Another landmark—the Government House—was the headquarters for Florida's Spanish governor. Its museum covers the city's Indian, European, and American pioneer history.

Henry Flagler built two grand hotels in St. Augustine. These ornate old structures are now the Lightner Museum and Flagler College. In the Fountain of Youth Archaeological Park, visitors can drink from the legendary spring.

North Central Florida

The Florida Museum of Natural History in Gainesville is part of the University of Florida. It is the largest natural history museum in the southeastern United States. The university is also proud of its zoo—and its Florida Gators football team.

Paynes Prairie Preserve covers 18,000 acres (7,284 ha) south of Gainesville. It used to be a lake, but all the water went down a hole called the Alachua Sink. In 1871, when the sink became clogged with logs, the prairie filled with water and became Alachua Lake. Then in the summer of 1891, the drain unclogged. Within a month, the lake had run dry.

Now bison, wild horses, and scrub (wild) cows trot across the grassy prairie where fish used to swim. The wild horses are descen-

dants of those that sailed to Florida with the Spaniards. Cows on a seventeenth-century Spanish cattle ranch are the ancestors of the Paynes Prairie cows.

A boardwalk at Paynes Prairie Preserve

Horses, Springs, and Wilderness

The Ocala region—with its rolling hills and tall, mossy oaks—is horse country. Thoroughbred horses graze on acres of white-fenced farms carpeted in bluegrass. On some farms, the owners welcome visitors and give them tours.

Visitors take a boat tour of Silver Springs.

Silver Springs, east of Ocala, is a group of 214 springs. They spout about 5,000 gallons (18,900 l) of water a second—enough to fill more than 700 Olympic-size swimming pools a day. Early Tarzan movies and TV's *Sea Hunt* series were shot there. Visitors can tour Silver Springs in a glass-bottomed boat and see the hole far below where the spring water comes out. Cave divers

A Day at the Horse Farm

On a typical horse farm, the horses' day begins at about 6:00 A.M. After they have a nutritious breakfast of alfalfa, the trainer paces them around a track to prepare them for racing. Grooms wash the horses and brush them down. Twice a day, a veterinarian inspects them closely for injury and disease. More exercise, training, and meals fill out the horses' day. In the evening, they go back to their paddocks and sleep—usually standing up.

After their racing days are over, stallions (males) and mares (females) are kept for breeding. Breeders are carefully chosen by owners for their health, strength, and racing records. Breeding season is in the early spring of each year. Eleven months after insemination, the mare gives birth to her 100-pound (45-kg) foal.

January 1 is the birthday of all Thoroughbred racehorses, no matter when they were born. A yearling is a horse that has passed its first birthday. Yearlings are gently broken, or trained to accept a rider. At age two—after their second January 1 birthday—they are ready for the racetrack. ▪

Cave Diving—Not for Everyone

In the cave-diving world, caves and caverns have special meanings. A "cave" is a space that is reached by at least 130 feet (40 m) of underwater travel, or one in which there is no light. A "cavern" has at least some visible light.

Cave divers need special training before they take their spooky dives. They wear scuba gear with air tanks and carry powerful flashlights. Often they end up in underwater channels that are too narrow to turn around in. Other channels are completely dark, with nowhere to come up for air.

Divers learn to battle their own terror and claustrophobia, or fear of enclosed places. As any cave diver will tell you, it's not a sport for everyone. ■

have found the bones of prehistoric animals in the spring's underwater caverns.

Nearby Ocala National Forest is a vast wilderness and recreation area. Its stands of pine, cypress, and maple trees hide white-tailed deer, cottontail rabbits, and black bears. Marjorie Kinnan Rawlings's novel *The Yearling* is set in this forest. Her home, where she wrote the book, is a state park to the north.

Daytona Beach

Daytona Beach is a thin strip of land between the Atlantic Ocean and the Halifax River. Since the 1980s, it has been a hot spot for college students on spring break. But Daytona is best known for car racing. Daytona International Speedway hosts the Daytona 500 and other great races. Several local museums feature car and car-racing history.

Daytona's Jackie Robinson Ballpark was named after the baseball star who played there in the 1940s. The minor-league Daytona Cubs play there now. Daytona's Museum of Arts and Sciences houses a large collection of Cuban art, donated by former Cuban president Fulgencio Batista.

Orlando Area Theme Parks

Walt Disney World in Orlando is the biggest entertainment complex in the world. It encompasses three theme parks—the Magic Kingdom, EPCOT Center, and Disney-MGM Studios.

The killer whale show at Sea World

Other theme parks in the Orlando area are Universal Studios, Sea World, Gatorland, and Splendid China. At Universal Studios, younger kids enjoy an interactive show with the lovable dinosaur Barney. Older kids go for three-dimensional action movies and thrilling rides into earthquakes, shark attacks, and the future.

Killer whales leap through the air at Sea World. Spectators get a drenching at the finale—a big splash by the largest whale, weighing 10,000 pounds (4,536 kg). Shows at Gatorland include jumping alligators and alligator wrestling.

Splendid China, in Kissimmee, contains replicas of more than sixty Chinese land-

Walt Disney World

Walt Disney World's Magic Kingdom (above left) is divided into seven "lands." Adventureland offers cruises through the jungle and a pirate raid. In Frontierland, the Splash Mountain log ride ends with a 52-foot (16-m) drop. Tomorrowland's favorite attraction is Space Mountain, a terrifying roller coaster that runs in the dark. Main Street USA, Liberty Square, Fantasyland, and Mickey's Toontown round out the kingdom.

EPCOT (above right) stands for *E*xperimental *P*rototype *C*ity *O*f *T*omorrow. Walt Disney planned to make the EPCOT Center a model community where people actually lived. It ended up as two theme parks—World Showcase and Future World. World Showcase features the architecture, food, and entertainment of eleven countries. Future World highlights the latest in science and technology, including computer games and virtual-reality demonstrations. Each night visitors are treated to a spectacular laser and brilliant fireworks show.

Visitors to Disney-MGM Studios can watch real television, movie, and animation productions in progress. But the Twilight Zone Tower of Terror draws the biggest crowds. Guests suddenly find themselves in the Twilight Zone, where their elevator drops in terrifying free fall. ■

Walt Disney

Walter Elias Disney (1901–1966) was an animation artist and filmmaker. Movie audiences saw his first Mickey Mouse cartoons in 1928. His first feature-length films were *Snow White* (1937), *Pinocchio* (1940), and *Bambi* (1942). Disney opened Disneyland, the world's first theme park, in Anaheim, California, in 1955. He planned a second theme park—Walt Disney World in Orlando—but never got to see it. He died five years before it opened in 1971. Today there are Disneyland theme parks in Europe and in Tokyo, Japan. ■

marks in exquisite detail. They include the Forbidden City, the Imperial Palace, the Great Wall, and the Stone Forest of Yunan.

Space and Treasure Coasts

The Atlantic coast east of Orlando is called the Space Coast. This stretch of marshes, lagoons, and islands is the center of the nation's

How Jupiter Got Its Name

In the 1500s, the Indians living in this area were the Hobe (HOH-bay). Spaniards first spelled the name Jobe, then Jove. (In Spanish, *j* is pronounced like *h*, and *b* and *v* are pronounced the same.) When the British arrived in 1763, they thought the place was named for Jove, the highest god of Roman mythology. They changed the name to Jupiter, a more common name for Jove. The town of Hobe Sound, north of Jupiter, keeps the Indians' original name. ■

Shipwrecked Treasure

Countless Spanish treasure ships sank off the Florida coast. Their cargoes of gold and silver bars and coins are worth hundreds of millions of dollars. And there they lie, just waiting to be discovered. Coins from sunken ships sometimes wash ashore after a storm, and beachcombers find them by accident. Other loot, buried by pirates and shipwreck survivors, lies waiting in hidden nooks.

Florida's earliest known shipwreck rests off Emanuel Point in Pensacola Bay. The ship was part of a 1559 Spanish expedition to colonize Florida. Archaeologists have recovered more than 3,000 artifacts after exploring only one-fifth of the site.

Divers can explore real shipwrecks at Florida's underwater archaeological preserves. The Spanish treasure ship *Urca de Lima* sank off Fort Pierce during a hurricane in 1715. McLarty Treasure Museum at Sebastian Beach displays some of the artifacts recovered from the ship. Another explorable wreck is the *San Pedro*, wrecked in the Keys near Islamorada in 1733. ■

space program. John F. Kennedy Space Center sits on Merritt Island, between the mainland and Cape Canaveral. Most of that island, however, is a wildlife refuge.

Windover Dig is an archaeological site near Titusville. In 1984, the 8,000-year-old remains of 168 prehistoric people were discovered in a pond there. Because the bodies sank into the muddy bottom, they were well preserved.

South of the Space Coast is Florida's Treasure Coast. Shipwrecks left fabulous sunken treasures there. Divers still comb the ocean floor, hoping to uncover a hidden chest of gold doubloons. Some of the towns along the coast are Vero Beach, Fort Pierce, Stuart, and Jupiter. Lake Okeechobee is directly inland from these towns.

Masaryktown

The New York editor of a Czech newspaper founded Masaryktown, in Hernando County. He named the town after Tomás G. Masaryk, the first president (1918–1935) of Czechoslovakia. ■

Tampa Bay Area

Over on the Gulf side of the state, the Pinellas Peninsula curves around from the mainland to form Tampa Bay. In 1528, Pánfilo de

Tampa is Florida's third-largest city.

Narváez was the first Spaniard to sail into Tampa Bay. Later, Spanish fishers and early pioneers set up villages in the area.

When Henry Plant's railroad reached Tampa in the 1880s, it become a major shipping center. Today Tampa is Florida's third-largest city. Plant's luxurious Tampa Bay Hotel is now the Henry B. Plant Museum and home to the University of Tampa.

Visitors to Tampa's Florida Aquarium follow the route of a drop of water through the state. On the way, they travel through mangrove swamps, underwater caverns, sandy shores, and coral reefs.

Ybor City

Vincente Martínez Ybor, a Cuban immigrant, opened a huge cigar factory outside Tampa in 1886. The community that sprang up around it was Ybor City. Thousands of Cubans came to work there, as well as immigrants from Italy, Germany, and Spain. By the early 1900s, Ybor City was the cigar-making capital of the world. More than 150 cigar factories employed tens of thousands of workers. They sat at long tables rolling cigars by hand. Perched on a raised platform was a reader who read newspaper articles, stories, and poems to the workers. ■

Busch Gardens

Busch Gardens is an African theme park with the nation's fourth-largest zoo. Lions, zebras, and giraffes roam the park's Serengeti Plain as visitors coast through on a monorail.

The Hillsborough River winds through Tampa. Upstream, it meanders through a moss-draped wilderness of oak and cypress. Flocks of long-legged ibis wade in the shallows, while turtles, alligators, and wild hogs lurk along the shore.

St. Petersburg, on the Pinellas Peninsula, faces Tampa across the bay. Its new domed stadium hosts concerts, as well as football, hockey, and baseball games. The city is a thriving arts community, too. Its Salvador Dalí Museum draws visitors from around the world.

John Ringling

John Ringling (1866–1936) was one of five brothers who expanded their musical act into a circus. In 1907 they bought another circus, forming the Ringling Bros. and Barnum & Bailey Circus. John built a winter home in Sarasota in 1912, and his circus spent the winters nearby. ■

Down the Southwest Coast

Snooty the manatee is the main attraction at Bradenton's South Florida Museum. Weighing 800 pounds (363 kg), he's the oldest manatee born in captivity. Snooty's daily diet consists of 50 pounds (23 kg) of lettuce, carrots, and apples.

Gamble Plantation in Ellenton, near Bradenton, is the last remaining plantation house in south Florida. Inside is Florida's only Confederate memorial. It honors Confederate Secretary of State Judah P. Benjamin, who hid out at the mansion after the war.

Downtown Sarasota is full of art galleries. The city's taste for fine art began with circus owner John Ringling, who built Cà d'Zan, his winter home, there. The lavish mansion, with its sculpture garden and rose garden, is open for tours. The Ringlings' fabulous collection of European paintings can be seen at the John and Mable Ringling Museum of Art.

Marie Selby Botanical Gardens in Sarasota has the world's largest collection of orchids. It is also the only botanical garden in the world specializing in epiphytes, or air plants. Another museum for plant lovers is Sarasota's Museum of Botany and Fine Arts.

Flamingos and peacocks wander among tropical jungle foliage at Sarasota Jungle Gardens. The animal shows here include such bizarre acts as cockatoos riding bikes on high wires and alligators leaping into the air.

Inventor Thomas Edison built a home and laboratory in Fort Myers. The house is surrounded by trees and shrubs he imported from around the world. Edison used many of these plants in his inventions. The bamboo, for example, became filaments in Edison's lightbulbs, and wax for his early phonograph records came from the garden's beehives. Hundreds of Edison's inventions are on display in his home-turned-museum.

Bridges connect Fort Myers to Sanibel and Captiva Islands, whose beaches are famous for their variety of colorful seashells. Sanibel's Ding Darling National Wildlife Refuge is a mangrove "jungle" that shelters alligators and rare waterbirds. Farther down the coast is Naples, an entry point to Big Cypress Swamp and the Everglades.

The Southeast

Palm Beach is known as a home and playground for the rich and famous. Residents include families with hundred-year-old fortunes, as well as movie stars and other newly wealthy people. Tourists come to Palm Beach to people-watch and mansion-gaze. Many enjoy window shopping in the elegant boutiques along

Palm Beach is a beautiful and wealthy community.

Worth Avenue. Railroad magnate Henry Flagler discovered Palm Beach's beauty in the 1890s. His mansion, Whitehall, is now a museum.

After the movie *Where the Boys Are*, Fort Lauderdale became a party town for college students on spring break. By the late 1980s, the city had suffered enough. Spring-breakers were declared unwelcome, and Fort Lauderdale began rebuilding its image as a place for business, culture, and family recreation. City planners cleaned up the beachfront and built a performing arts center and an art museum.

Miami and Miami Beach

Miami, on the southeast coast, began as Fort Dallas in 1870. Today the city is a colorful mix of skyscrapers, pastel houses, and palm trees.

Brickell Avenue, once lined with millionaires' homes, is now Miami's financial district. Miami-Dade Public Library, the Center for the Fine Arts, and the Historical Museum of Southern Florida make up the massive Metro-Dade Cultural Center. A Spanish-style plaza connects the three buildings.

Overlooking Biscayne Bay is Villa Vizcaya, a lavish mansion with formal gardens and fountains. Industrialist James Deering built the 70-room villa—now a museum—in 1916.

Just west of downtown is Little Havana, a vibrant Cuban neighborhood that centers around *Calle Ocho* (Eighth Street). Cuban restaurants, groceries, and shops line the streets, and venerable old men play dominoes in the park. More than a million people gather in Little Havana for Carnaval, its springtime festival. Other ethnic neighborhoods are Little Managua, named for the capital of the South American country of Nicaragua, and Little Haiti.

Bahamians founded the community of Coconut Grove in 1840. By the 1890s, Europeans and Americans had moved in, too. In the 1960s, it was a haven for artists, writers, and intellectuals. Today Coconut Grove is a funky, fashionable neighborhood of shops, cafés, and celebrities' mansions.

Miami is a city of diversity and contrasts.

Buildings in the south suburb of Coral Gables are modeled after the architecture of Spain. The Biltmore Hotel, an example of the original architecture, is still open.

Across Biscayne Bay, causeways and bridges connect Miami with Miami Beach. Situated on a narrow, sandy island, Miami Beach has one industry—tourism. Almost 2 million visitors arrive every year. On the south end is trendy South Beach. Farther up the island is sophisticated Bal Harbour and residential Golden Beach.

The Spanish monastery at North Miami Beach is the oldest building in the Western Hemisphere. It was built between 1133 and 1141 in Seville, Spain. Newspaperman William Randolph Hearst had it taken apart, packed in boxes, and shipped to the United States in 1928. Only in 1954—after Hearst died—were the pieces unpacked, sorted, and the monastery rebuilt.

The Spanish monastery in North Miami Beach

South Dade

Exotic animals and plants inhabit South Dade, or southern Dade County. They live in Parrot Jungle, Monkey Jungle, Orchid Jungle, Fruit and Spice Park, and Miami Metrozoo.

More than a thousand tropical birds live in Parrot Jungle. Parrots, cockatoos, and macaws do tricks at the trained-bird shows. In Monkey Jungle, visitors walk through the cages of free-roaming monkeys. Monkey Jungle takes part in an international program to breed wild animals and then release them into protected habitats.

The Metrozoo, a cageless zoological park, is one of the best zoos in the world. Riding the monorail, people can glimpse white Bengal tigers, lowland gorillas, and other African and Asian animals.

The Florida Keys

An early Spanish explorer named these islands *Los Martires* (The Martyrs) because they looked like a row of suffering men. The Overseas Highway (U.S. Highway 1) runs the length of the Florida Keys. Its 42 bridges span 15 percent of the highway's total length. Locations along the road are expressed by mile-marker (MM) numbers. They begin with MM Zero in Key West and end at MM 112 north of Key Largo.

Spectacular coral reefs run the length of the Keys. One of the best spots to explore is John Pennecamp Coral Reef State Park on Key Largo. Besides reefs, the park has mangrove swamps and a beach. Visitors can take glass-bottomed boat tours or go snorkeling or sailing. At the Wild Bird Rehabilitation Center, people can see rescued injured birds and feed fish to Rembrandt, a great white heron.

Tropical birds are the main attraction at Parrot Jungle.

Visitors can feed the dolphins at the Dolphin Research Center on Grassy Key.

Islamorada (Purple Island) was named for its violet-colored sea snails. Off the coast is the San Pedro Underwater Archaeological Park, where a Spanish fleet sank in 1733.

At the midpoint of the Keys is a group of islands called the Marathon Keys. Marathon Key itself is a modern city with its own airport. Nearby Grassy Key is the home of the Dolphin Research Center. Pigeon Key served as a work camp for men who built the Seven-Mile Bridge between Marathon Key and Little Duck Key. The bridge was part of Henry Flagler's railroad to Key West.

Wildlife thrives in the untouched woods of the Lower Keys. The National Key Deer Refuge and Great White Heron National Wildlife Refuge are located on Big Pine Key. The best time to catch a glimpse of the Key deer is in the early morning or late evening.

Key West

Key West has long been a refuge for artists, writers, and people who just want to "get away from it all." Author Ernest Hemingway lived and wrote there. So did John James Audubon, who saw his first great white heron in the Florida Keys. President Harry Truman spent vacations at his "Little White House" on Key West. Their homes are now museums, and their lives are just a few of the local legends.

A trolley rattles through the historic quarter of Old Town, with its brightly painted nineteenth-century homes. People can also tour the sites on the old-time Conch Train or take the Writers' Walk past famous authors' homes.

After a few days in Key West's charming, laid-back atmosphere, visitors are ready to agree with Truman: "This place is all that I'd hoped it would be."

Ernest Hemingway lived and wrote in this house in Key West.

"Today's the Day!"

That was Mel Fisher's cheery motto every morning for sixteen years in his quest for the *Atocha.* Loaded with 40 tons of treasure, the Spanish galleon had gone down in a hurricane off the Florida Keys in 1622.

July 20, 1985, *was* the day— the day Mel's crew at last uncovered the *Atocha.* Its treasures were beyond Mel's wildest dreams. They are considered the richest find since the discovery of King Tut's tomb in Egypt in 1922. The priceless cargo included chests of jewels, gold and silver coins, and stacks of silver bars.

Mel (below) started dreaming of sunken treasure as a boy, while reading pirate tales and Robert Louis Stevenson's *Treasure Island.* At age eleven, he took his first dive—in a muddy Indiana lagoon. A lifetime of treasure diving led to the *Atocha* find. Mel is still diving for treasure. To him, the quest is more thrilling than the discovery.

Mel Fisher's Treasure Museum in Sebastian displays artifacts from a Spanish fleet wrecked in 1715. Visitors are also welcome at the Mel Fisher Maritime Heritage Society Museum in Key West. It houses both sunken artifacts and research labs to study and preserve them. ■

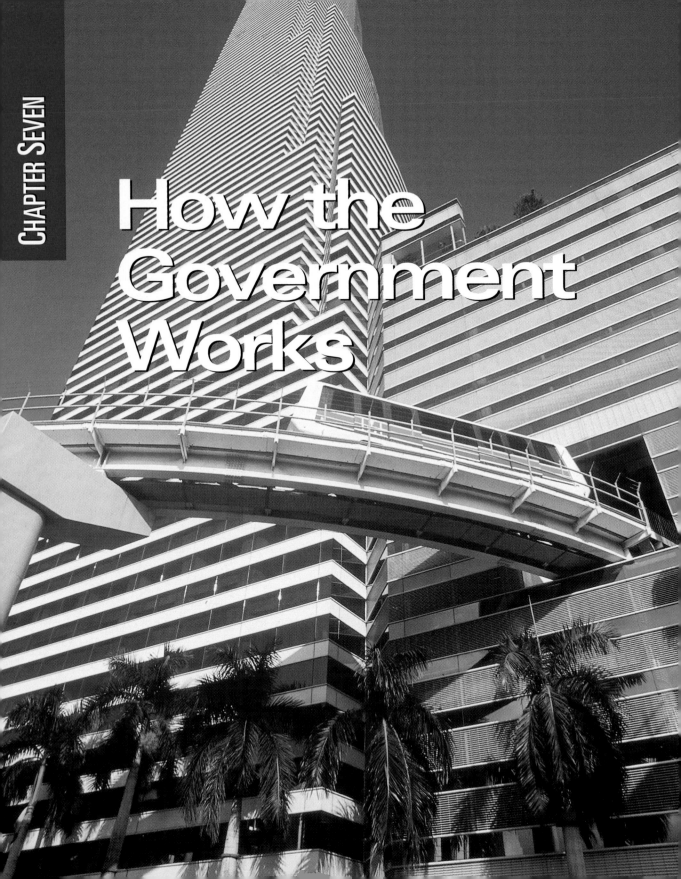

CHAPTER SEVEN

How the Government Works

Governor Lawton M. Chiles Jr. addresses a joint session of the Senate and House at the state capitol.

All eyes are glued to the giant scoreboard at the front of the room, with its red and green blinking lights. Down below in their seats, people squirm and sweat as they tally the lights—some delighted, others clearly annoyed.

No, it's not a racetrack or a stock exchange. It's the Florida state legislature taking a vote! As each member's name is called, they press one of two buttons mounted on their desks—a green button to vote yes or a red one to vote no. Then a colored light blinks on as the board registers their votes.

The tale is told of one representative who didn't like to sit through the voting process. He'd jam a conch shell onto his voting button to register a constant yes and then take off.

How Wishes Become Laws

The light show can be exciting, but it doesn't happen every day. Voting takes place only after a long chain of events. In Florida, a bill becomes a state law in much the same way as a bill in the U.S. Congress becomes a federal law.

Let's say that a group of people wants a certain law to be passed. First, they persuade their state legislator—either a senator or a representative—that it's a good idea. He or she agrees to sponsor the idea and introduces it. Once the proposal is written out properly, filed, and given a number, it's called a "bill."

Opposite: The Government Center and Metromover in Miami

A Tale of Two Capitols

Florida's state capitol is a 22-story marble skyscraper in downtown Tallahassee. Only three other state capitols are skyscrapers: those of Louisiana, Nebraska, and North Dakota.

The sleek new capitol, (above left) which opened in 1977, houses the legislature and the offices of the governor and cabinet members. Murals of historic scenes decorate the first floor, and paintings by modern Florida artists are also on display. The House and Senate chambers are on the fifth floor. Visitors can watch their lawmakers in action from the observation deck.

Florida's old capitol (above right) was in service for 135 years. Some officials wanted to tear it down after 1977, but preservationists won their battle to save it. Built in 1842, it was remodeled in the early 1900s. Today it looks as it did a century ago—with red-striped awnings and a silver dome. In the old days, the Senate and House occupied opposite ends of the building. The Supreme Court, governor, and cabinet members also had offices there.

Today state history exhibits occupy several offices in the old building. Exhibits in the Supreme Court chamber describe important law cases of the past. Samples of state symbols are also on display—moonstone, agatized coral, and a stuffed Florida panther. ■

Next, a committee and a specialized subcommittee examine the bill. It may bounce back and forth among committees, perhaps being rewritten several times. Then it goes to the rules committee. Plenty of bills are stacked up at this stage, but only those placed on the calendar reach the legislature for discussion.

Once it comes before the legislators, the bill may go through several amendments, or changes. When it reaches its final form, members debate the bill's good and bad points. Finally, it's time for a vote. Voting takes place by roll call—one by one, names are called and buttons are pushed. The "scoreboard" starts blinking. In the end, if at least half the lights are green, the bill has passed that house of the legislature.

Now the battle is only half over. If the bill started in the House of Representatives, it moves on to the Senate—where this same process begins again. The Senate may pass the bill, but with a few more amendments. Then it's back to the House again for approval. Once both houses have approved the bill, it becomes an "act."

Next, the governor has seven working days in which to sign or veto (reject) the act. In some states, an act dies if the governor takes no action. But Florida's constitution keeps this from happening. If the governor does nothing, the act becomes a law after seven days.

Of course, the governor may still veto the act. In that case, it takes a two-thirds' vote in both chambers of the legislature to override the veto and make a new law.

The Lawmakers

Florida's state government is set up just like the U.S. government. Power is divided among three branches of government—legislative, executive, and judicial. The three branches keep a check on one another, so that there's always a balance of power.

As in the U.S. Congress, the Florida legislature is bicameral, or composed of two houses—a Senate and a House of Representatives. The 40 state senators and 120 state representatives are Florida's lawmakers. They are elected from districts mapped out according to the number of residents.

In area, some districts are tiny and others are huge. Every ten years, after the U.S. government takes a census, Florida reapportions (redraws) its legislative districts. This ensures that people in all areas of the state are fairly represented.

State legislators may serve for up to eight years in a row. Senators are elected to four-year terms and may be reelected once. Every two years, half the Senate seats are up for reelection. Representatives, with two-year terms, may stay in office for up to four terms.

The legislature opens its regular, sixty-day session in early February. If there is important business to take care of, the session may be extended or a special session may be called.

The Executives

The governor is the head of the executive branch of government. This branch has the power to carry out state laws. Both the governor and the lieutenant governor are elected to four-year terms and may serve a maximum of two terms.

Six other people—the cabinet members—hold high executive posts. They include the secretary of state, attorney general, and commissioners of agriculture and education. The governor appoints

Governor Chiles, with middle school students, announcing that a cigarette billboard would be removed

Florida's Governors

Name	Party	Term	Name	Party	Term
Thomas Brown	Whig	1849–1853	Sidney J. Catts	Prohib.	1917–1921
James E. Broome	Dem.	1853–1857	Cary A. Hardee	Dem.	1921–1925
Madison S. Perry	Dem.	1857–1861	John W. Martin	Dem.	1925–1929
John Milton	Dem.	1861–1865	Doyle E. Carlton	Dem.	1929–1933
Abraham K. Allison	Dem.	1865	David Sholtz	Dem.	1933–1937
William Marvin	None	1865	Fred P. Cone	Dem.	1937–1941
David S. Walker	Cons.	1865–1868	Spessard L. Holland	Dem.	1941–1945
Harrison Reed	Rep.	1868–1873	Millard F. Caldwell	Dem.	1945–1949
Ossian B. Hart	Rep.	1873–1874	Fuller Warren	Dem.	1949–1953
Marcellus L. Stearns	Rep.	1874–1877	Daniel T. McCarty	Dem.	1953
George F. Drew	Dem.	1877–1881	Charley E. Johns	Dem.	1953–1955
William D. Bloxham	Dem.	1881–1885	LeRoy Collins	Dem.	1955–1961
Edward A. Perry	Dem.	1885–1889	C. Farris Bryant	Dem.	1961–1965
Francis P. Fleming	Dem.	1889–1893	W. Haydon Burns	Dem.	1965–1967
Henry L. Mitchell	Dem.	1893–1897	Claude R. Kirk Jr.	Rep.	1967–1971
William D. Bloxham	Dem.	1897–1901	Reubin O. Askew	Dem.	1971–1979
William S. Jennings	Dem.	1901–1905	Bob Graham	Dem.	1979–1987
Napoleon B. Broward	Dem.	1905–1909	Wayne Mixson	Dem.	1987
Albert W. Gilchrist	Dem.	1909–1913	Bob Martinez	Rep.	1987–1991
Park Trammell	Dem.	1913–1917	Lawton M. Chiles Jr.	Dem.	1991–

department heads to oversee the environment, transportation, labor, and many other areas.

The Courts

The judicial branch of government interprets the laws. Judges in the court system base their decisions on the constitution and state laws.

Florida's seven-member Supreme Court is the state's highest court. It meets in Tallahassee, in a building opposite the west face of the capitol. A nominating committee proposes candidates for the Supreme Court, and the governor appoints members from this group. Justices serve six-year terms. Every two years, they select one of their members to serve as chief justice.

Beneath the Supreme Court are five district courts of appeal. Judges in the state's twenty circuit courts preside over most of the serious law cases. Each of Florida's counties has at least one county court.

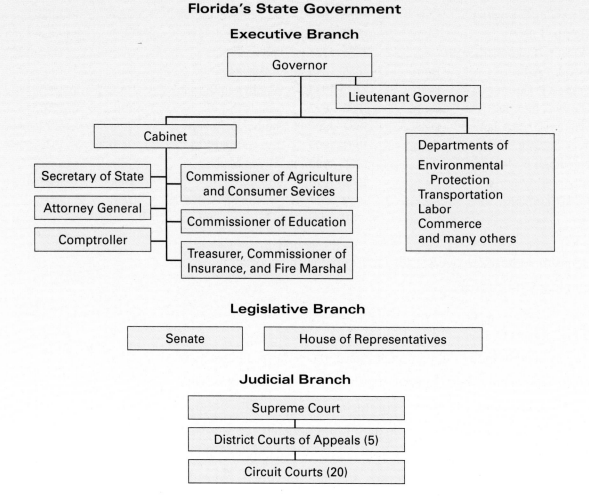

Florida's State Government

Executive Branch

Governor

Lieutenant Governor

Cabinet

Secretary of State

Attorney General

Comptroller

Commissioner of Agriculture and Consumer Sevices

Commissioner of Education

Treasurer, Commissioner of Insurance, and Fire Marshal

Departments of

Environmental Protection
Transportation
Labor
Commerce
and many others

Legislative Branch

Senate

House of Representatives

Judicial Branch

Supreme Court

District Courts of Appeals (5)

Circuit Courts (20)

The Constitution—Keeping Up with Modern Times

Florida's first constitution was drawn up in 1839, before Florida became a state. Among other things, it declared that no one who had taken part in a duel could hold public office. Later constitutions were adopted in 1861, 1865, 1868, and 1885.

Today's state constitution went into effect in 1969. It is about 38,000 words long—almost twice as long as this book! But the 1885 constitution was even longer. With all the additions through its 33-year history, it grew to 50,000 words. (Compare that to the U.S. Constitution, which is only about 6,000 words long.)

No other state has a chance to change its constitution the way Florida does. Every twenty years, a special commission reviews the constitution to see if it needs any changes. This is a good idea because the state is growing and changing so fast. Commissioners study current issues and hold public hearings before they make recommendations. Then the suggested changes go directly to the citizens for a vote. The year 1998 was the last review year before the twenty-first century.

Between reviews, there are other ways to make amendments, or changes, to the constitution. Legislators may propose an amendment. Then both houses of the legislature must approve the change by a three-fifths vote. Next, a majority of Florida's voters must approve it. Or, using the "initiative" process, citizens may start a petition for an amendment. In this case, the people—not the legislators—vote to pass the amendment. Citizens may also start a petition to hold a constitutional convention.

Counties, Cities, and Towns

Florida started out with only two counties—Escambia and St. Johns. They were established on July 21, 1821—four days after Florida became a U.S. territory. Today the number of counties has grown to sixty-seven.

In most counties, a five-member board of commissioners heads the county government and presides over a group of county commissioners. These commissioners are elected by voters in each of the county's districts.

What If the Voters Say No?

In the 1978 constitutional review, voters rejected all the commission's proposed amendments. Their work was not wasted, however. As time went on, people had a chance to think about some of the proposals. In later years, they voted to adopt many of them. Some were introduced by the initiative process, and others began in the legislature. ■

Florida's counties

Janet Reno

Janet Reno (1938–) is the first female attorney general of the United States. President Bill Clinton appointed her in 1993, and she served during his two terms in office. Born in Miami, she moved to a home near the Everglades when she was eight years old. There she enjoyed horseback riding, camping, and scuba diving. Reno received her law degree from Harvard University in 1963 and was appointed Dade County State's Attorney in 1978. Voters elected her for four more terms. As U.S. attorney general, she focused on children involved in gangs and drugs, repeat criminals, civil rights, and environmental issues. ■

The State Flag

Spain, France, Great Britain, the United States, and the Confederate States of America have all flown their flags over Florida. Voters approved today's official state flag in 1899. It features two red bars that cross in the form of an X on a white background. The state seal is in the center, where the bars cross. ■

The State Seal: Getting It Right

The state seal combines symbols of Florida's history, wildlife, and industry: a Seminole woman, a sabal palm tree, and a steamboat under the rays of the rising sun.

Florida has changed its state seal several times. The legislature set up a basic design in 1868. But early versions contained a few mistakes. The

steamboat seemed to be sinking. The Indian woman wore the feathered headdress of a male Plains Indian. In the foreground was a sack of coffee—not an important Florida crop. And in the background were mountains—landforms that Florida does not have!

One by one, through the years, the mistakes were corrected. The last change, in 1970, transformed the coconut palm into a sabal palm. ■

Florida's State Symbols

State animal: Florida panther In 1982, students in Florida voted on the state animal. They chose the Florida panther, the state's most endan-

gered animal. This light-brown, 6-foot (1.8-m) -long cat is one of the few cougar species left in the United States. It lives in the Everglades and Big Cypress, preying on deer and other mammals. It joined the federal endangered list in 1967 and became a state endangered species in 1973.

State bird: Mockingbird Mockingbirds live in Florida all year long. They sing cheery, rambling melodies, often late into the night. As their name suggests, they can also mimic

other birds' songs. Both the male and the female build the nest, and their eggs are blue-green with brown spots. Mockingbirds are fiercely protective parents. People or animals who wander too close to a mockingbird's nest are likely to be dive-bombed!

State flower: Orange blossom Spaniards brought orange trees to Florida in the 1500s. When the trees are in bloom, their white flowers fill the air with a heavy, sweet fragrance.

State tree: Sabal palm Sabal palm trees are native to Florida and grow all over the state. They take root in almost any type of soil. Early settlers nicknamed them "cabbage palms" because their crunchy buds taste like cabbage.

State marine mammal: Manatee The Florida coast is the best place in the United States to see the endangered manatee. Homesick sailors used to mistake manatees for mermaids. Their flippers, seen from far away, can look a little like hands. (The name "manatee" comes from the Latin word *manatus,* meaning "having hands.")

State saltwater mammal: Porpoise Porpoises have super eyesight and hearing but no sense of smell. They navigate using echolocation. It works like this: They send out sounds, and the sound waves bounce off objects in the water. The returning sound waves tell the porpoise how close, how large, and how dense the object is. Porpoises use barks and whistles to communicate with one another. Scientists rank them between dogs and chimpanzees in intelligence.

State butterfly: Zebra longwing Zebra longwings (above) are commonly seen in southern Florida, especially in Everglades National Park. They live with their relatives in flocks. Each individual has its favorite "perch," where it returns to sleep every night.

State saltwater fish: Sailfish Sailfish can swim as fast as 60 miles (100 km) an hour. They migrate to Florida for the winter as more northerly Atlantic water gets cold. Sailfishing is one of Florida's most popular sports.

State reptile: Alligator Alligators live in Florida's wetlands. Like other cold-blooded animals, they often stretch out in the open to bask in the sun. Florida law bans feeding alligators—it makes them lose their fear of humans. Females lay thirty to fifty eggs, and the newly hatched babies are about 8 inches (20 cm) long.

State freshwater fish: Largemouth bass The Florida bass, a largemouth bass, weighs up to twice as much as its cousins in northern states. It is black with a wide mouth and a notch in its dorsal, or back, fin. The female lays as many as 25,000 eggs at once, and they hatch in a few days.

State stone: Agatized coral You can find agatized coral in Tampa Bay and in the riverbeds of the Econfina and Withlacoochee-Suwannee rivers. It took 20 million to 30 million years to form these stones. Regular coral consists of skeletons of tiny sea creatures called coral polyps. The coral became "agatized" through the years as silicon replaced the calcium in the skeletons. ■

Florida's State Song

"The Swanee River" (also known as "Old Folks at Home")

Words and music by Stephen C. Foster (1851)
Foster's original version was written in African-American dialect. Also, the river in Florida is spelled Suwannee, not Swanee.

Verse 1
*'Way down upon the Swanee
    River,
Far, far away,
There's where my heart is
    turning ever,
There's where the old folks stay.
All up and down the whole
    creation
Sadly I roam,
Still longing for the old
    plantation,
And for the old folks at home.*

Chorus
*All the world is sad and dreary,
Everywhere I roam;
Oh, brothers, how my heart
    grows weary,
Far from the old folks at home!*

Verse 2
*All 'round the little farm I
    wandered
When I was young,
Then many happy days I
    squandered,*

*Many the songs I sung.
When I was playing with my
    brother
Happy was I;
Oh, take me to my kind old
    mother!
There let me live and die.*
(Chorus)

Verse 3
*One little hut among the bushes,
One that I love,
Still sadly to my memory
    rushes,
No matter where I rove.
When will I see the bees a-
    humming
All 'round the comb?
When will I hear the banjo
    strumming,
Down in my good old home?*
(Chorus)

Counties have many other elected officials. They include a county clerk, a state's attorney, a sheriff, and a coroner.

In cities and towns, a mayor or a city manager is the chief executive. As with the county government, voters elect people to represent them in the city council.

A Tax-Free State

Florida is one of the few states whose residents pay no state income tax. The state government collects the money it needs through other types of taxation, such as sales taxes. That money supports public schools, public housing, state parks, highways, and medical and social services.

CHAPTER EIGHT

Floridians at Work

This tour guide in the Florida Everglades is one of the millions of service workers in Florida.

"Of all Americans who took travel vacations in the last five years, a stunning 63.8 percent vacationed in Florida at least once." That's what *Florida Trend* magazine reported in 1995. More than 51 million tourists visited Florida that year, up from 20 million in 1980.

Tourism is Florida's biggest industry. That's one reason why services make up 81 percent of the gross state product (GSP). More than 3 million Floridians—55 percent of the labor force—work in the service industries. For example, the person in the Mickey Mouse suit at Walt Disney World is a service worker. Other service workers have jobs in hotels, resorts, and national parks.

Retired people use another large segment of services. Building their homes keeps real estate and construction workers busy. Insurance, banking, farm labor, and public education all come under the heading of services.

Florida's economy is growing faster than that of almost any other state. Tourism keeps growing, and older people keep pouring

Opposite: One of Florida's many orange-packing factories

Kennedy Space Center

The Kennedy Space Center tests and launches all U.S. space shuttles and other spacecraft. Visitors can watch spectacular liftoffs from the space center. The nearby space museum exhibits everything from moon rocks and space-suits to *Apollo* and *Gemini* space capsules and full-sized replicas of moon modules, Mars craft, and space shuttles. Eight rockets used in early space shots stand in the Rocket Garden outside.

Next to the museum is the Galaxy Theater. Its four IMAX screens show five-story-high movies filmed from space shuttles. At the Astronaut Hall of Fame, west of the space center, visitors can whirl around in a centrifuge to experience simulated spaceflight firsthand. ▪

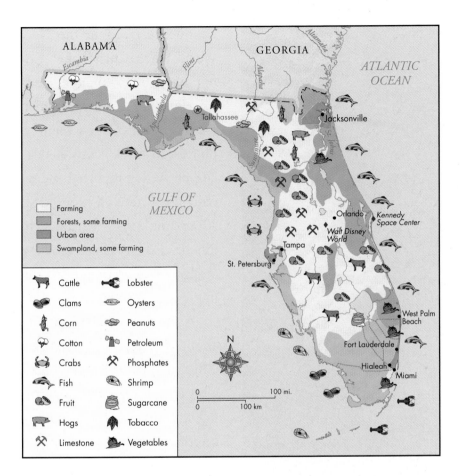

Florida's natural resources

Map legend:

Farming
Forests, some farming
Urban area
Swampland, some farming

Cattle · Lobster
Clams · Oysters
Corn · Peanuts
Cotton · Petroleum
Crabs · Phosphates
Fish · Shrimp
Fruit · Sugarcane
Hogs · Tobacco
Limestone · Vegetables

Map labels: ALABAMA, GEORGIA, ATLANTIC OCEAN, Tallahassee, Jacksonville, GULF OF MEXICO, Orlando, Kennedy Space Center, Walt Disney World, Tampa, St. Petersburg, West Palm Beach, Fort Lauderdale, Hialeah, Miami

What Is the Gross State Product?

First, let's talk about goods and services. "Goods" are actual objects that Florida sells, such as orange juice, telephones, and phosphate rock. "Services" are helpful efforts that people pay others to provide. Doctors, store clerks, and tour guides are among Florida's service workers. If you add up all the money that was paid for these goods and services in a year, you get Florida's gross state product. ■

in to spend their later years in the sunshine. More and more companies are deciding to relocate in Florida. The federal government plays a part in the state's economy, too. It employs thousands of people on military bases and at the Kennedy Space Center.

Five Hundred Years of Citrus Fruit

Citrus fruits originated in Southeast Asia and the East Indies. Traders brought them to India, then to the Mediterranean region.

Oranges arrived in the New World when Christopher Columbus brought orange seeds to Haiti in 1493. Spanish explorers introduced them in Florida. In 1579, Pedro Menéndez de Avilés reported seeing wild citrus trees all over the St. Augustine area. Farmers in Pinellas County began growing oranges as a commercial crop in the early 1800s.

Agriculture makes up only about 3 percent of Florida's GSP. But one-third of the state's land area is devoted to farming. Oranges are the most important crop. Most of the orange groves are in south-central Florida, west of Orlando. Florida is the world's second-largest producer of oranges and orange juice, after Brazil.

Grapefruits, tangerines, lemons, and limes are also important citrus crops. Florida's first grapefruit seeds were planted in 1825. Today Florida leads the world in grapefruit production. About one-third of the world's grapefruit—and 84 percent of the U.S. grapefruit crop—comes from Florida. Yellowish-green Key limes are also valuable for their juice and for the oils in their skin.

In 1992, Hurricane Andrew devastated much of south Florida's fruit crop. Thousands of orange, grapefruit, and tangerine trees were destroyed. Around the country, citrus fruit prices skyrocketed because the supply was so low. Growers were able to save some trees, but many groves had to be replanted.

Many other tropical fruits grow in southern Florida's balmy climate. These include bananas, avocados, mangoes, papayas, litchi fruit, guavas, passion fruit, and kumquats.

When winter sweeps across the northern states, Florida ships them vegetables fresh from the fields. They include tomatoes, potatoes, sweet corn, cabbage, celery, cucumbers, and green peppers.

Lush sugarcane fields south of Lake Okeechobee make Florida the nation's top sugarcane state. Florida and California take turns as the leader in potted plants, ferns, and other greenhouse products. Florida's livestock farms raise beef and dairy cattle, hogs, pigs, and chickens.

When Is a Crop Not a Crop?

You may think of crops as farm products. But once they're processed into another form, they're considered factory items. In Florida, processed food is a big business. Processing plants turn out citrus juice, canned fruit, frozen vegetables, jelly, and hundreds of other foods.

Orange Juice

Orange juice is Florida's official state beverage. More than 90 percent of Florida's oranges are processed into orange juice. Florida's own Department of Citrus scientists invented frozen concentrated orange juice in 1945. Today about four-fifths of Florida's juice output is frozen concentrate.

What happens to the rest of the orange after the juice is squeezed out? The leftover pulp is used for animal feed. Citrus flavoring, molasses, and jelly are some other by-products of orange-juice processing. ■

Opposite: Oranges are the most important crop in Florida.

Manufacturing accounts for 10 percent of Florida's GSP. The only factory goods that outdo foods are communications equipment. Telephones, broadcasting equipment, and military communications devices are just a few examples. Factories for these products are centered around Tampa and Fort Lauderdale.

Fisheries and Mines

Florida's fishers haul in whatever people will eat, including sharks and octopuses. They catch menhaden, too, but no one eats it. This member of the herring family is used for bait or turned into fertilizer, fish oil, or cattle food.

Shrimp, lobsters, and scallops are the most valuable catches in Florida's waters—10 percent of the nation's shrimp comes from Florida. Red snapper, grouper, mackerel, oysters, and crabs are

Opposite: A shrimp boat casts out along the Tampa coast.

among the major saltwater species. The main freshwater catch is catfish, which thrive in Lake Okeechobee and the St. Johns River.

In Hamilton County and the Tampa area, miners dig out rich deposits of phosphate rock. These mines provide about 80 percent of all the phosphate rock in the United States. Much of it is processed into fertilizer.

Most of Florida's petroleum comes from wells in Santa Rosa County. Limestone quarries provide materials for building roads and making cement. Other Florida minerals include fuller's earth (a clay for processing petroleum), kaolin (pottery clay), thorium, and zircon.

John Gorrie

John Gorrie (1803–1855), a doctor from Apalachicola, is called the "father of air conditioning and refrigeration." He invented an air-cooling machine to lower his patients' temperatures. Gorrie's method is still used in refrigerators today. His statue stands in Statuary Hall in Washington, D.C. ■

What Florida Grows, Mines, and Manufactures

Agriculture	Mining	Manufacturing
Oranges and other citrus fruits	Phosphate rock	Electrical and electronic equipment
Tomatoes and other vegetables	Petroleum	Processed food
Greenhouse and nursery products	Natural gas	Scientific instruments
Beef cattle		Printed materials
		Chemicals

Getting There—and Getting Around

Looking for a safe way to get through the Everglades? Take Alligator Alley, also known as Interstate 75. It cuts across the big, spooky swamp, offering all the scenery but none of the dangers.

Florida works hard to keep up with traffic. In 1965, 3.5 million vehicles were registered in the state. By 1992, there were 11.2 million—not counting all the out-of-state visitors. By the mid-1990s, Florida had built about 113,000 miles (181,856 km) of roads and highways. In the Keys, people can drive all the way to Key West on the Overseas Highway.

Railroads gave Florida its first big economic boom a century ago. Rail travel isn't as important today—most people use cars and airplanes instead. But passenger and freight trains still link many Florida cities.

Foreign visitors fly into Miami International Airport (one of the busiest airports in the United States), as well as Tampa International and Orlando International airports. Passenger and cargo terminals handle heavy traffic to and from South America. Major airlines also fly into Fort Lauderdale, West Palm Beach, Fort Myers, Jacksonville, and Sarasota-Bradenton.

Florida has fifteen deepwater ports that handle international cargo ships. The largest and busiest is the port of Tampa.

The Seven-Mile Bridge in the Lower Keys

Spreading the Word

William Charles Wells of St. Augustine published Florida's first newspaper—the *East Florida Gazette*—in 1783. It came out just in time to report the colonists' victory in the Revolutionary War. Wells wasn't too happy about the news, however, because he had wanted the British to win. He closed down his paper the same year it began, when England gave Florida back to Spain.

Today the oldest newspaper in the state is Jacksonville's *Florida Times-Union,* established in 1864. Other major daily papers are the *Miami Herald,* the *Tampa Tribune,* the *Orlando Sentinel,* the *St. Petersburg Times*, and the *Tallahassee Democrat.* The *Miami Herald* publishes both an English and a Spanish edition.

WQAM, Florida's first radio station, started broadcasting from Miami in 1921. Miami's WTVJ-TV first went on the air in 1949.

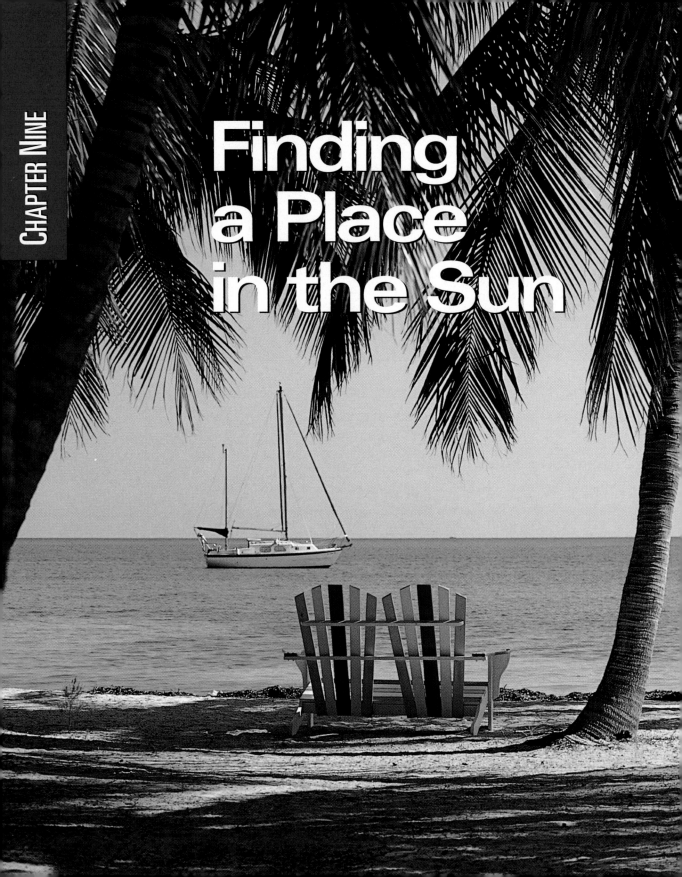

CHAPTER NINE

Finding a Place in the Sun

A sunny afternoon in St. Augustine

Most people in the Sunshine State came from somewhere else. Out of every five residents, only one was born in Florida. Others have come to work, to find freedom, or to retire. For many, Florida is an international port of entry into the United States. About one out of seven Floridians was born in another country.

Florida's population is the fourth-largest among the states, after California, New York, and Texas. Florida is also the fourth-fastest-growing state. Between 1970 and 1995, its population more than doubled—from 6.8 million to 13.9 million. Florida officials expect to see a population of 15.4 million by the year 2000.

Where People Live

If the people of Florida were spread evenly across the state, there would be 222 people per square mile (86 per sq km). That's more than two football fields per person. But the people are actually spread out very *un*-evenly. Nine out of ten people live in the state's metropolitan areas.

Jacksonville is Florida's largest city, followed by Miami, Tampa, and St. Petersburg. This gives the impression that there's plenty of elbow room between big population centers. But if you look at counties instead of cities, you get quite a different picture.

In 1900, two-thirds of Florida's population lived in the north. By mid-century, the bulk of population was clustered in the

Opposite: A sailboat anchored off the Florida Keys

Florida's Amazing Growth

Year	Population	Rate of Growth
1950	2,771,305	
1960	4,951,560	79%
1970	6,789,443	37%
1980	9,746,324	44%
1990	13,003,362	33%
2000	15,415,135 (est.)	19%

Population of Florida's Major Cities (1990)

Jacksonville	672,971
Miami	358,548
Tampa	280,015
St. Petersburg	238,629
Hialeah	188,004
Orlando	164,693

southeastern counties. At the end of the twentieth century, Dade County (Greater Miami), Broward County (Fort Lauderdale area), and Palm Beach County are the most heavily populated. Almost one-fourth of all Floridians live in Dade and Broward counties.

A Cluster of Cultures

About one-eighth of Florida's people are Hispanic, including almost half of Miami's population. Most Hispanics speak Spanish at home. Cubans, the largest Hispanic group in the state, built Ybor City, near Tampa, into the cigar-making capital of the world in the 1880s. Miami's Little Havana neighborhood sprang up after the Cuban revolution of 1959. Other Hispanics came from Nicaragua, Honduras, Guatemala, Colombia, and Peru.

Blacks represent about 14 percent of Florida's population. Most are African-Americans descended from slaves, who made up almost 50 percent of the state's population in the 1840s.

Another group of blacks came from Haiti, Jamaica, and the Bahamas. Many refugees from Haiti, the fastest-growing group, live in the Little Haiti area of northeastern Dade County and in Coral Springs. Haitians speak a Creole language— a mixture of French, Spanish, English, and Portuguese, as well as various African and American Indian languages.

Bahamians founded the south Florida community of Coconut Grove in 1840. Every summer, in lavish costume, they celebrate their roots with the Goombay Festival. The Black Heritage Museum in Dade County traces the history of Jamaicans, Bahamians, Haitians, and African-Americans in the Miami area.

Children of many cultures attend Florida's schools.

Transplanted Traditions

Florida's Jewish community looks back on a history of almost 500 years in the region. The earliest Jewish settlers arrived with Ponce de León. Driven from Spain because of their religion, they hoped to find a land where they could live in peace and freedom.

In the 1930s, Jewish families from northern states began moving into Miami Beach. By 1947, half the city's residents were

What Are Crackers, Anyhow?

Natives of Florida are called "Crackers," but no one is sure why. The most common story is that cattle herders in the 1800s were named Crackers for the sound of their cracking whips. But the British used the same name for Maryland backwoodsmen. Some say the name comes from "corn-crackers," a British nickname for poor Southerners, who supposedly lived on corn.

Not everyone likes being called a Cracker. To some, it suggests simple country folk. Others are proud of the Cracker tradition. Cracker houses have become a well-known style of Florida architecture. The earliest examples were pioneers' one- or two-room log cabins. Later Cracker farmhouses were more often square with a covered porch and a pointed roof. ■

Jewish. Exhibits in the Ziff Jewish Museum of Florida in Miami Beach portray centuries of Jewish life in the state.

A thriving Greek community centers around Tarpon Springs. Immigrants arrived in the early 1900s to dive for sponges. Now the city is the world's largest supplier of natural sponges. Residents

Cuban Culture in American Life

Pop singer Gloria Estefan (right), actor Andy Garcia, fashion model Albita—these are just a few of the well-known figures who share a Cuban heritage.

Cuban culture is firmly fixed in American popular culture. The mambo and the cha-cha have their dance-floor diehards, and Cuban cigars are known as the finest in the world. Cuban cuisine is a restaurant specialty in big cities all over the country. The Cuban film *Strawberry and Chocolate* was nominated for an Academy Award. Another movie, *The Perez Family*, brought a struggling Cuban family to the screen. Old Cuban postcards have even become prized collectors' items.

In the 1940s and 1950s, Cuba's capital of Havana was the culture and entertainment center of the Caribbean. Its glamorous hotels, resorts, and casinos drew an international crowd. With the 1959 revolution, however, the fiesta came to an end. Since then, Cuban exiles have continued to make their traditions a part of American life. ■

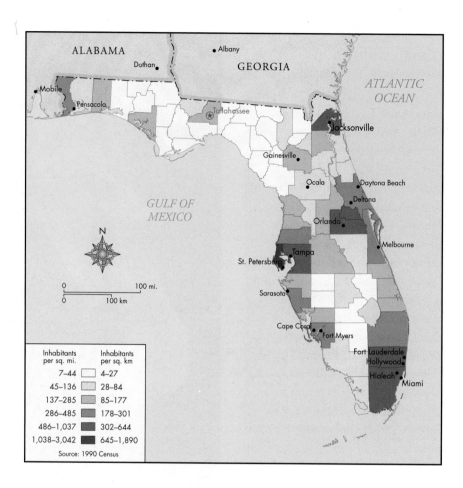

Florida's population density

follow the traditions of the Greek Orthodox Church. Their festivals are exuberant occasions for Greek music, dancing, and food.

The Oldest Floridians

According to the 1990 census, about 42,000 Native Americans live in Florida. Most live and work in white society, however. Only about 2,000 Seminole and 500 Miccosukee live on Florida's Indian reservations.

Both Native American groups earn money from craft sales, cultural shows, and various businesses. Some Seminole reservations, for example, are working cattle ranches. The income provides schooling and social services for the people.

Traditional Seminole and Miccosukee houses are called *chickees*. Sturdy cypress poles support a roof of thatched palmetto leaves, leaving the sides open to the air. In a traditional Seminole family camp, several chickees are arranged in a group—one for cooking, one for sleeping, one for socializing, and so on. Frybread, sofkee, and beef jerky are typical Seminole foods.

Some Seminoles still perform their traditional Stomp Dance and Green Corn Dance. Others preserve the arts of making dugout canoes, practicing herbal medicine, making patchwork crafts, and weaving palmetto and sweet grass baskets. Seminole language and legends have practically vanished, however. Chief James Billie of the Bird Clan does his best to keep them alive. The singer and storyteller spins his tales at the annual Florida Folk Festival.

At Miccosukee Indian Village in the Everglades, residents demonstrate beadwork and patchwork and maintain a museum. Their bare-handed alligator-wrestling shows are more than just a tourist attraction. The Miccosukee once caught alligators for food. They tied the 'gators' legs together to keep them from escaping before mealtime.

Farmers and Cowboys

In Florida's rural north, some farm families still live as their pioneer ancestors did, plowing their fields with draft horses instead of tractors. After the harvest, they can fruits and vegetables. Sugar-

Farming is a way of life in Florida's rural north.

cane farmers grind cane on horse-powered mills and boil the juice to make syrup.

White Springs hosts the Florida Folk Festival in the spring and Rural Folklife Days in the fall. Exhibitors demonstrate pioneer crafts such as blacksmithing and making bent-cypress furniture, lye soap, and quilts.

Big-brimmed hats, tooled leather boots, and fancy belt buckles—Florida's cowboy culture is hard to miss. Cattle and horses sailed to Florida with the Spaniards in the 1500s. Today Florida's biggest cattle ranches cover tens of thousands of acres. Cowboys show off their bronco-riding and steer-wrestling skills at rodeos in Arcadia, Davie, and Kissimmee.

Growing Old in the Sun

Florida is a warm and pleasant place for people to spend their retirement years. In fact, people over age eighty-five make up the fastest-growing age group in Florida. Florida ranks first in the United States in the percentage of residents who are sixty-five or older. Almost 20 percent of the population fits into this category.

Many people retire to Florida.

Hundreds of Years of Schools

The oldest wooden schoolhouse in the United States stands in St. Augustine's historic district. It was built in the 1500s by Spanish missionaries, who set up Florida's first schools. The mission schools taught religion and Spanish to American Indians and settlers' children. Later, British colonists set up private schools in Pensacola and St. Augustine. Free public education began with the constitution of 1868.

Today, more than 2.3 million students are enrolled in Florida's public elementary and high schools. Attendance is required from age six through sixteen. About 43 percent of these students are minorities with black, Hispanic, Asian, or American Indian backgrounds. Students who aren't proficient in English are entitled to bilingual classes.

The oldest wooden schoolhouse in the United States is in St. Augustine.

More than 50,000 children in the state attend private schools. They range from Montessori preschools to military academies and church-supported high schools.

Florida has more than 39 accredited four-year colleges and universities. About one-third are state-supported, and the others are private. The department of education also operates community colleges and vocational schools throughout the state.

Mary McLeod Bethune

Mary McLeod Bethune (1875–1955) taught at mission schools in Florida from 1895 to 1904. In 1904, she opened the Daytona Normal and Industrial Institute for Girls. This school merged with Cookman Institute in 1923 and was renamed Bethune-Cookman College. Bethune was the director of the National Youth Administration's Division of Negro Affairs as well as the founder and first president of the National Council of Negro Women. ▪

Key Lime Pie

Key limes are small, yellow citrus fruits native to southern Florida. A Key West cook named Sarah is said to have invented the recipe for Key lime pie. Here is one version.

Ingredients:

- 15-oz. can of condensed milk
- 1 tablespoon grated Key lime rind
- 1/2 cup Key lime juice
- 1/4 teaspoon salt
- 4 eggs
- 4 tablespoons sugar
- 1 graham cracker piecrust

Directions:

Separate the egg yolks and whites. Mix together the egg yolks, condensed milk, rind, lime juice, and salt. Beat until thick.

In a separate bowl, mix the egg whites and sugar. Beat until the mixture is thick enough to stand up in peaks.

Fold about one-third of the egg whites into the lime mixture, and pour it into the pie crust.

Swirl the rest of the egg whites on top.

Bake at 350°F for 15 to 20 minutes or until lightly browned.

Chill before serving. (True Key lime pie is yellow, not green!)

CHAPTER TEN

Culture and Fun

Cyclists love Florida because it's so flat. Surfers ride the waves, and fishers angle for "the big one." Artists love the scenery, and writers find a refuge. The Sunshine State is best known as a place to have fun, but culture flourishes there, too. Florida hosts the most college football bowl games in the United States, but it also has the most art museums. In fact, Florida spends more of its state budget on the arts than any other state except New York.

Surfing, sunning, and sailing at Fort Lauderdale

A Sport for Every Taste

Florida's coasts and inland waterways are great locations for water sports. Some of the favorites are surfing, windsurfing, snorkeling, scuba diving, waterskiing, jet skiing, sailing, canoeing, and fishing.

In state and national parks, bike paths wind through forests and swamps. Roller-skating and inline skating are the rage along beachfront sidewalks and malls. Serious skaters can find miles of smooth, traffic-free asphalt paths along the southeast coast.

Florida is a top spot for year-round golfing, with many public golf courses. Florida also hosts several major golf tournaments every year. Tennis is wildly popular, too. Native tennis champ Chris Evert gave the sport a boost in the 1970s and 1980s. Tennis camps, schools, and resorts around the state give players a chance to train with pros.

Opposite: A shopping area in Coconut Grove

Chris Evert

Christine Marie Evert (1954–), professional tennis champion, was born in Fort Lauderdale. She began playing tennis at age five and went on to win 157 tournament titles, including 18 Grand Slams. From 1975 to 1981, she was ranked the world's number-one tennis player six times. Evert retired in 1989 and lives in Boca Raton. She was inducted into the Tennis Hall of Fame in 1995. ■

Team Sports

Florida sports fans are rooting for more and more new professional teams. In professional basketball, the Miami Heat began its first season in 1988. The Tampa Bay Devil Rays opened their first Major League Baseball season in 1998. St. Petersburg remodeled its ThunderDome into Tropicana Field for the occasion. In 1995, Jacksonville welcomed its own professional football team—the Jacksonville Jaguars. They play home games in Jacksonville Municipal Stadium, the former Gator Bowl.

The Florida Marlins (affectionately called the "Fighting Fish" by their fans) came into existence as an expansion team in 1993. In 1997, they shot up in the standings after a major free-agent spending spree by their owner, entertainment magnate H. Wayne Huizenga. This brought All-Stars and Florida natives Alex Fernandez and Gary Sheffield to the team. The Marlins shocked the baseball world by defeating the Cleveland Indians in the 1997 World Series. They had become baseball's "youngest" team ever to win the championship—after only four years in existence. South Florida went wild over the team's success. The Latino community had an overnight hero in Livan Hernandez, a Cuban who had defected to the United States.

Hernandez became the ace of the Marlins' pitching staff in the playoffs and the World Series.

The Miami Dolphins, Florida's oldest professional football team, have played in the Super Bowl five times. In 1972, they set a record with the only undefeated season in National Football League history.

Florida hosts more college football bowl games than any other state in the country. The best-known games are held in the Orange Bowl in Miami, the Citrus Bowl in Orlando, and the Jacksonville Municipal Stadium.

Major League Baseball teams with spring-training camps in Florida make up the Grapefruit League. Fans all over the country come down for their exhibition games in February and March.

Florida played a part in the 1996 Summer Olympic Games, held in Atlanta, Georgia. Miami's Orange Bowl and Orlando's Citrus Bowl were regional sites for the soccer games.

Dan Marino

Daniel Constantine Marino III, Miami Dolphins quarterback, is the National Football League's champion pass-thrower. Marino leads the NFL in touchdowns, yardage, pass attempts, and pass completions. ■

The Orange Bowl in Miami

Florida's Professional Sports Teams

Team	League	Home Stadium
Florida Marlins	Major League Baseball	Pro Player Stadium, Miami
Tampa Bay Devil Rays	Major League Baseball	Tropicana Field, St. Petersburg
Miami Heat	National Basketball Assn.	Miami Arena
Orlando Magic	National Basketball Assn.	Orlando Arena
Miami Dolphins	National Football League	Pro Player Stadium, Miami
Tampa Bay Buccaneers	National Football League	Tampa Stadium
Jacksonville Jaguars	National Football League	Jacksonville Municipal Stadium
Florida Panthers	National Hockey League	Miami Arena
Tampa Bay Lightning	National Hockey League	The Ice Palace, Tampa

Speed Sports

In 1956, a horse named Needles was Florida's first Kentucky Derby winner. That really kicked off the state's racehorse craze. Florida breeds about 9 percent of the nation's racehorses—some 5,000 Thoroughbreds—a year. But more than 20 percent of the winners in sweepstakes races are from Florida. Two popular racetracks are Miami's Hialeah Park and Hallandale's Gulfstream Park, home of the Florida Derby.

Greyhound dog racing is another Florida sport. Florida has more dog racetracks than any other state.

Daytona calls itself the Birthplace of Speed. National and international car and motorcycle races heat up its famous speedway every year. Other racetracks serve the Miami area, Tampa, Gainesville, Pensacola, and dozens of other cities.

Daytona International Speedway

Car racing on the beach was getting to be a big problem for Daytona. That's why the city built Daytona International Speedway in 1959. When the races are on, 85,000 roaring spectators crowd into the grandstands. Another 50,000 fans camp on the grassy infield.

The wildly popular Speed Weeks are held before the Daytona 500 in February. Cars speed around the 2.5-mile (4-km) track at close to 200 miles (322 km) an hour. Turns are slanted at a 30-degree angle to keep the speeding cars from flying off the track. Off season, the speedway is whisper-quiet. Occasionally, turtles from a nearby pond wander onto the dusty track. ■

Jai Alai

Why is jai alai called the world's fastest game? Because the *pelota* (ball) whizzes by at speeds of up to 175 miles (282 km) an hour.

Jai alai originated in the Basque region of Spain. Today it's a popular sport throughout Spain, France, Italy, Mexico, and South America. Basques brought it to Cuba, then it made its way to Miami. *Jai alai* means "merry festival" in the Basque language.

In Florida, professional players compete in *frontons,* or arenas, before thousands of spectators. Games are played on a three-walled court. Players wear a *cesta* (curved wicker basket) on one hand to whack a hard ball of goatskin-covered rubber against the wall. The object is to hurl the ball in such a way that the opponent cannot return it, either in the air or after the first bounce. ■

James Weldon Johnson

James Weldon Johnson (1871–1938), born in Jacksonville, was a lawyer, statesman, and author. "Lift Every Voice and Sing," written with his brother John, is known as the black national anthem. Johnson served as U.S. consul to Venezuela and Nicaragua and executive secretary of the National Association for the Advancement of Colored People (NAACP). ■

Another Florida "speed" sport is jai alai (pronounced HI-lie). This exciting handball game is called the fastest game in the world. Miami Jai Alai is the oldest *fronton* (jai alai arena) in the country.

The "Write" Place

When he was a boy, Billy Bartram took a trip to Florida. Later he wrote *Travels through North and South Carolina, Georgia, East and West Florida.* Published in 1791, Billy's book stirred up international excitement about Florida. It's said that the book inspired Samuel Taylor Coleridge to write his enchanting poem "Kubla Khan."

Florida tales appear in the works of Washington Irving, James Fenimore Cooper, and Stephen Crane. Crane's *The Open Boat*

Marjorie Kinnan Rawlings

Marjorie Kinnan Rawlings (1896–1953) was a writer who lived on a farm on Cross Creek in central Florida. Many of her stories describe the lives of Florida's early pioneers. Her best-known novel, *The Yearling,* won the 1939 Pulitzer Prize and was made into a movie. Rawlings enjoyed hunting and fishing.

Guests at her farm included writers such as Ernest Hemingway and F. Scott Fitzgerald. Her Cracker-style home at Cross Creek is now a state historic site. ■

Zora Neale Hurston

Zora Neale Hurston (1903–1960), an African-American anthropologist and writer, was born in Eatonville. In the 1930s, Hurston worked closely with the Harlem Renaissance, an African-American arts movement. She became the nation's most important compiler of African-American folklore. Hurston's stories explore life in Florida's rural black communities. Her 1937 novel *Their Eyes Were Watching God* takes place in Eatonville. ■

describes his harrowing shipwreck off the Florida coast. Harriet Beecher Stowe, author of *Uncle Tom's Cabin,* spent winters near Jacksonville. In *Palmetto Leaves* (1873), she celebrated the beauty of the St. Johns River region.

Florida's climate and scenery attracted famous writers such as Ernest Hemingway, Tennessee Williams, and Marjorie Kinnan

Isaac Bashevis Singer

Isaac Bashevis Singer (1904–1991) wrote novels, short stories, and plays. He taught at Miami University and lived in Miami Beach, which he called the "city of the future." In tales such as "Yentl" and "The Magician of Lublin," Singer wrote about life in the Jewish communities of his native Poland. He won the Nobel Prize for literature in 1978. ▪

Rawlings. Sarasotan John D. MacDonald set his mystery thrillers in Miami, the Everglades, and other Florida spots.

Today, some of the state's resident writers are novelists Ralph Ellison and Thomas McGuane, Haitian poet Felix Morrisseau-Leroy, and humorist Dave Barry.

Performing Arts

Most big cities in Florida have their own symphony orchestra. The Florida Philharmonic Orchestra, based in Fort Lauderdale, plays in several area cities. In college towns, chamber music and choral groups enrich the classical music scene. Miami Beach's New World Symphony is composed of young adults. Every summer, the Sarasota Music Festival welcomes young musicians from all over the world to study and play.

In 1965, opera star Luciano Pavarotti made his first U.S. appearance with the Greater Miami Opera. Founded in 1941, it was the first of the state's seven opera companies. Miami's Florida Grand Opera takes its productions to cities around south Florida. The Miami City Ballet, founded in the 1970s, performs in both Miami and Naples. More than thirty other professional dance troupes perform throughout Florida.

Florida has an official state play—*Cross and Sword*, by Paul Green. With lavish costumes and rousing music, it dramatizes the Spaniards' colonization of St. Augustine. Florida has over thirty theater companies, too. They include the Pope Theater Company in Palm Beach, the Phoenix Production Company in Melbourne, and Florida Studio Theater in Sarasota.

Sidney Poitier

Sidney Poitier (1927–), movie actor, was born in Miami. He won an Academy Award in 1963 for his role in *Lilies of the Field*. *Guess Who's Coming to Dinner* (above, with Poitier on the left) and *In the Heat of the Night* are some of his other films. ■

On the popular music scene, south Florida throbs to the beat of Cuban and Caribbean music. The Jacksonville Jazz Festival hosts international jazz stars every October.

The Artists' State

The exotic Everglades and historic St. Augustine were favorite subjects for artists in the 1800s. Boston artists Winslow Homer and William Morris Hunt painted Florida landscapes. John James Audubon traveled as far as Key West to study and sketch local birds for his *Birds of America* engravings.

"Cannonball" Adderley

Julian ("Cannonball") Adderley (1928–1975) was one of the world's greatest jazz saxophonists. Born in Tampa, he started his first jazz band when he was a high-school student in Tallahassee. After two years with Miles Davis's band, he formed his own quintet, known for its "soul jazz" style. A passionate player with a charming personality, Adderley appeals to fans around the world. ■

Salvador Dalí

Salvador Dalí (1904–1989) was a Spanish artist who painted fantastic, dreamlike scenes. His style is called *surrealism*, meaning "beyond realism." Well-known images in Dalí's paintings include a watch "melting" over the edge of a box.

Dalí gave his works whimsical names such as *Telephone in a Dish with Three Grilled Sardines at the End of September*. The man was as peculiar as his paintings. He kept a pet elephant and was known to sport a several-foot-long mustache and wear a loaf of bread for a hat. ■

Florida has more than thirty art museums and dozens of art galleries—more than any other state. Wealthy art lovers stirred up interest in the arts by donating their collections to museums. The John and Mable Ringling Museum of Art in Sarasota is a treasurehouse of Renaissance and Baroque paintings. The Salvador Dalí Museum in St. Petersburg holds the world's largest collection of Dalí's works. They are gifts of textile designer Reynolds Morse and his wife, Eleanor.

Black artists called the Highwaymen started painting Florida scenery in the 1950s. Many were amateurs who learned by experimenting. Their name comes from the way they sold their work—by loading up the car and cruising the highways for buyers. If they

The Art Deco District

Miami Beach's Art Deco district has the biggest collection of Art Deco–style buildings in the world. Hundreds of them are clustered in the South Beach area between Ocean Avenue and Lennox Drive. The earliest were built in the 1930s with local limestone and stucco. Facades, grillwork, porches, and etched glass sported flamingo, tropical flower, and sun-ray designs. Other buildings featured porthole-shaped windows and steamship smokestacks. Aztec and Egyptian themes added an exotic flair.

The district became increasingly run-down until the 1970s, when preservation and restoration began. The entire area became a National Register Historic District in 1979. Today more than 600 buildings are officially protected. Many of the original white exteriors are now pink, blue, salmon, lime green, and other tropical pastels. ■

got ten or fifteen dollars for a painting, they were happy. Now collectors pay thousands of dollars for the Highwaymen's vibrant landscapes.

Ethnic and Folk Arts

Florida's ethnic and folk arts are the best reflection of the state's diverse culture. Seminole and Miccosukee Indians make bracelets and bead necklaces, baskets woven of pine needles and grass, and handwoven clothing. The Miccosukee are famous for their patchwork sewing with its brilliantly colored designs. Traditional Seminole crafts include cow-whips, moccasins, and dolls.

Paintings by Cuban and other Hispanic artists hang in the Florida Museum of Hispanic and Latin American Art, in Miami's Buena Vista neighborhood. Cuban craftspeople are known for their woodcarvings and embroidered shirts called *guyaberas*. Handmade boats and sails are a Caribbean specialty, while the people of Florida's Greek community are known for making diving and seafaring gear.

Bent-cypress furniture, lye soap, and quilts are traditional crafts of Florida's rural farm communities. They show their skills every year during the Florida Folk Festival and Rural Folklife Days in White Springs.

Florida's Division of Historical Resources offers apprenticeship programs in ethnic and folk arts. Masters in each craft are matched up with students who want to learn them.

The Historical Museum of Southern Florida

At Miami's Historical Museum of Southern Florida, the Tropical Dreams exhibit is a walk through time. It explores the lives of Florida's people from prehistoric times until today. Artifacts include the Paleo-Indian tools of early hunters, silver bars from Spanish treasure hunts, a 1930s Miami streetcar, and Haitian refugee rafts. Full-size plates of Audubon bird pictures are among the museum's prized collections. Young people can take part in music, dance, and other cultural programs. On walking tours and boat tours, patrons explore Miami communities such as Little Havana and Coconut Grove. ■

These programs have covered an amazing array of arts and crafts: Indian patchwork, African-American gospel music and singing, "Cracker" cow-whip making, Haitian and Jamaican story-telling, Everglades skiff-building, Anglo-American fiddle-playing, and Japanese dance. It's a fine testimony to all the people—past and present—who came to Florida and stayed to enrich it.

Timeline

United States History

Florida State History

1513 The Spanish explorer Juan Ponce de León lands on the coast of Florida.

1539 Hernando de Soto lands at Tampa Bay.

1565 Spanish colonists establish St. Augustine, the first permanent European settlement in what is now the United States.

1607 The first permanent British settlement is established in North America at Jamestown.

1620 Pilgrims found Plymouth Colony, the second permanent British settlement.

1763 Spain cedes Florida to Great Britain.

1776 America declares its independence from England.

1783 Treaty of Paris officially ends the Revolutionary War in America.

1783 Florida is returned to Spain by Great Britain after the American Revolution

1787 U.S. Constitution is written.

1803 Louisiana Purchase almost doubles the size of the United States.

1812–15 U.S and Britain fight the War of 1812.

1817 The First Seminole War begins.

1819 Spain cedes Florida to the United States.

1822 Florida becomes a U.S. territory.

1824 Tallahassee is made territorial capital

United States History

The North and South fight **1861–65** each other in the American Civil War.

The United States is **1917–18** involved in World War I.

Stock market crashes, plunging the **1929** United States into the Great Depression.

The United States fights in **1941–45** World War II.

The United States becomes a **1945** charter member of the United Nations.

The United States fights **1951–53** in the Korean War.

The U.S. Congress enacts a series of **1964** groundbreaking civil rights laws.

The United States **1964–73** engages in the Vietnam War.

The United States and other **1991** nations fight the brief Gulf War against Iraq.

Florida State History

1835–42 The Second Seminole War forces resettlement of most Native Americans to Oklahoma Territory.

1845 Florida becomes a state.

1861 Florida secedes from the Union and joins the Confederacy.

1868 Florida is readmitted to the Union.

1926 Florida's real estate boom collapses.

1949 A missile test center is established at Cape Canaveral.

1961 First manned U.S. capsule is launched from Cape Canaveral.

1969 Florida's sixth constitution is adopted.

1992 Hurricane Andrew devastates southern Florida.

Fast Facts

A young girl feeds the seagulls.

Statehood date	March 3, 1845, the 27th state
Origin of state name	Named *Pascua Florida* (Flowery Easter) by Ponce de León on Easter Sunday, 1513
State capital	Tallahassee
State nickname	Sunshine State
State motto	"In God We Trust"
State animal	Florida panther
State beverage	Orange juice
State freshwater fish	Florida largemouth bass
State saltwater fish	Atlantic sailfish
State bird	Mockingbird
State flower	Orange blossom
State butterfly	Zebra longwing
State gem	Moonstone
State stone	Agatized coral
State song	"The Swanee River," also known as "Old Folks at Home"
State tree	Sabal palm
State fair	Tampa (early to mid-February)

Zebra longwing

Northern panhandle

Jacksonville's
Riverwalk

Total area; rank	59,988 sq. mi. (155,368 sq km); 22nd
Land; rank	53,997 sq. mi. (139,851 sq km); 26th
Water; rank	5,991 sq. mi. (15,517 sq km); 7th
Inland water; **rank**	4,683 sq. mi. (12,129 sq km); 4th
Coastal water; **rank**	1,308 sq. mi. (3,388 sq km); 6th
Geographic center	In Hernando County, 12 mi. (19 km) northwest of Brooksville
Latitude and longitude	Florida is located approximately between 24° 30' and 31° N and 80° and 87° 38' W
Highest point	In Walton County, 345 feet (105 m)
Lowest point	Sea level along Atlantic Ocean
Largest city	Jacksonville
Number of counties	67
Longest river	St. Johns River, 275 miles (443 km)
Population; rank	13,003,362 (1990 census); 4th
Density	222 persons per sq. mi. (86 per sq km)
Population distribution	85% urban, 15% rural

Ethnic distribution		
(does not equal 100%)	White	83.0 %
	African-American	13.6 %
	Hispanic	12.17%
	Asian and Pacific Islanders	1.19%
	Other	1.48%
	Native American	0.28%

Record high temperature	109°F (44°C) at Monticello on June 29, 1931
Record low temperature	–2°F (–19°C) at Tallahassee on February 13, 1899

Everglades

Average July temperature	81°F (27°C)
Average January temperature	59°F (15°C)
Average yearly precipitation	54 inches (137 cm)

Castillo de San Marcos

De Soto National Memorial

Florida's Natural Areas

National Parks and Preserves

Everglades National Park is a vast wilderness covering the southern tip of the Florida Peninsula.

Big Cypress National Preserve adjoins the Everglades.

Biscayne National Park is a series of small islands in Biscayne Bay, south of Miami.

Dry Tortugas National Park is about 65 miles (105 km) west of Key West.

National Seashores

Canaveral National Seashore is a preserved area north of Kennedy Space Center.

Gulf Islands National Seashore lies south of Pensacola.

National Historical Monuments and Memorials

Castillo de San Marcos National Monument (St. Augustine) is the oldest masonry fort in the United States.

De Soto National Memorial (Tampa) commemorates Hernando de Soto and his landing in Florida in 1539.

Fort Caroline National Memorial (Jacksonville) is near the site of the second French fort in the United States.

A cypress grove

National Forests

Apalachicola National Forest is in the Florida Panhandle and contains beautiful swamps, rivers, and lakes

Ocala National Forest is a huge wilderness area of pines and swamps.

Osceola National Forest is the smallest national forest in Florida.

State Parks

Florida has 110 state parks. They include John Pennekamp Coral Reef State Park (95 percent of which is under water) and Myakka River State Park (the largest state park in Florida). Florida's state forests cover a total of 16.5 million acres (6.7 million ha).

Sports Teams

NCAA Teams (Division 1)

Bethune-Cookman College Wildcats

Florida A&M University Rattlers

Florida Atlantic University Owls

Florida International University Golden Panthers

Jacksonville University Dolphins

Stetson University Hatters

University of Central Florida Knights

University of Florida Gators

University of Miami Hurricanes

University of South Florida Bulls

Major League Baseball

Florida Marlins

Tampa Bay Devil Rays

The Orange Bowl

Chris Evert

National Basketball Association

Orlando Magic

Miami Heat

National Football League

Jacksonville Jaguars

Miami Dolphins

Tampa Bay Buccaneers

National Hockey League

Florida Panthers

Tampa Bay Lightning

Cultural Institutions

Libraries

The St. Augustine Free Public Library is the oldest library in Florida, having opened in 1874.

The State Library of Florida (Tallahassee) has noted collections on Florida's history.

The P. K. Yonge Library of Florida History (University of Florida) owns an outstanding collection of books about the state.

Museums

The John and Mable Ringling Museum of Art (Sarasota) is noted for its Baroque art collection.

The Florida Museum of Natural Resources at the University of Florida (Gainesville) houses the noted Key Marco Collection of Native American artifacts.

The Salvador Dalí Museum (St. Petersburg) exhibits Dalí's surrealist art.

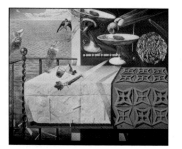

A Salvador Dalí painting

The Museum of Florida History (Tallahassee) has wide-ranging displays on Florida's rich past.

Performing Arts
Florida has than thirty dance companies, more than thirty professional theater companies, seven major symphony orchestras, and seven opera companies.

Universities and Colleges
In the mid-1990s, Florida had 39 public and 69 private institutions of higher learning.

Annual Events

January–March
Greek Epiphany Ceremony in Tarpon Springs (January 6)

Old Island Days in Key West (January–March)

Black Hills Passion Play in Lake Wales (mid-February through Easter)

Florida Citrus Festival in Winter Haven (February)

Florida State Fair in Tampa (February)

Swamp Buggy Days in Naples (February)

Festival of States in St. Petersburg (March)

Flying High Circus in Tallahassee (March)

Motorcycle Week in Daytona Beach (March)

Ringling Museum's Medieval Fair in Sarasota (March)

April–June
De Soto Festival in Bradenton (April)

Easter Week Festival in St. Augustine (April)

Fiesta of Five Flags in Pensacola (May)

Florida Folk Festival in White Springs (May)

Muccosukee craftswoman

Daytona International Speedway

International Festival in Miami (May)

Pensacola Shark Rodeo in Pensacola (June)

Cross and Sword Official State Play in St. Augustine (June–July)

July–September

Rodeos in Arcadia and Kissimmee (Fourth of July weekend)

Firecracker 400 Auto Race in Daytona Beach (Fourth of July)

Days in Spain in St. Augustine (August)

October–December

Beaux Arts Promenade in Fort Lauderdale (November)

Gator Bowl Festival and Football Game in Jacksonville (December or January)

Blockbuster Bowl Football Game in Miami (December or January)

Florida Citrus Bowl Football Game in Orlando (last week in December or first week in January)

Famous People

Mary McLeod Bethune

"Cannonball" Adderley (1928–1975)	Jazz musician
John James Audubon (1785–1851)	Artist and ornithologist
Mary McLeod Bethune (1875–1955)	Educator and reformer
Steve Carlton (1944–)	Baseball player
Jacqueline Cochran (1910?–1980)	Aviatrix and businesswoman
Faye Dunaway (1941–)	Actor
Chris Evert (1954–)	Tennis player
Henry Morrison Flagler (1830–1913)	Industrialist and developer
John Gorrie (1803–1855)	Physician and inventor
Zora Neale Hurston (1901–1960)	Writer
James Weldon Johnson (1871–1938)	Writer and educator

Osceola

Edmund Kirby-Smith (1824–1893)	Confederate army officer
Osceola (1804?–1838)	Seminole leader
Sidney Poitier (1927–)	Actor
A. Philip Randolph (1889–1979)	Labor Leader
Marjorie Kinnan Rawlings (1896–1953)	Writer
John Ringling (1866–1936)	Circus entrepreneur
John Stilwell (1883–1946)	U.S. Army general
Clarence Thomas (1948–)	Supreme Court justice

To Find Out More

History

- Derr, Mark. *Some Kind of Paradise: A Chronicle of Man and the Land in Florida.* New York: William Morrow & Co., 1989.

- Fradin, Dennis B. *Florida.* Chicago: Childrens Press, 1992.

- Jahoba, Gloria. *Florida: A History.* New York: W. W. Norton & Co., 1984.

- Morgan, Cheryl K. *The Everglades.* Mahwah, N.J.: Troll, 1990.

Fiction

- Rawlings, Marjorie Kinnan. *The Yearling.* New York: Collier Macmillan Publishers, 1967.

Biographies

- Anderson, Peter. *John James Audubon: Wildlife Artist.* New York: Franklin Watts, 1995.

- McKissack, Patricia, and Frederick L. McKissack. *Mary McLeod Bethune.* Chicago: Childrens Press, 1992.

Websites

■ **Florida Kids' Page**
http://www.dos.state.fl.us/kids/
A guide to Florida's museums, rural life, shipwreck sites, and other cultural and historical information.

■ **NASA Shuttle Status**
http://www.jsc.nasa.gov/pao/media/mstat/current.html
Gives up-to-the-minute reports on space shuttle operations, including docking missions with Russian space station *Mir*. Also tells how to get mission reports sent directly to you via e-mail.

■ **Florida Keys National Marine Sanctuary**
http://www.fknms.nos.noaa.gov/
Provides information on the ecology, marine life, and history of the Florida Keys.

Addresses

■ **Florida Division of Tourism**
126 West Van Buren Street
Tallahassee, FL 32399-2000
(904) 487-1462
For information about travel in Florida

■ **Museum of Florida History**
R. A. Gray Building
500 S. Bronough Street
Tallahassee, FL 32399-0250
(904) 487-2299
For information about Florida history

Index

Page numbers in *italics* indicate illustrations

Meet the Author

Ann Heinrichs fell in love with faraway places while reading Doctor Dolittle books as a child. She has traveled through most of the United States and several countries in Europe, as well as northwest Africa, the Middle East, and east Asia.

Ann first dug her bare toes into the squeaky sands of Fort Walton Beach at age 12. She first met the Atlantic Ocean on Florida's eastern shore. "Trips are fun, but the real work—tracking down all the factual information for a book—begins at the library. I head straight for the reference department. Some of my favorite resources are statistical abstracts and the library's computer databases.

"For this book, I also read magazines and newspapers from several Florida cities, as well as issues of *Florida Heritage* magazine. Talking with Florida residents gave me more local details. The

Internet was a super research tool, too. Florida has some of the most complete websites I've ever seen on state history, culture, and government.

"To me, writing nonfiction is a bigger challenge than writing fiction. With nonfiction, you can't just dream something up— everything has to be researched. I study government reports, analyze statistics tables, and then try to give the information a human face." Ann Heinrichs grew up in Arkansas and lives in Chicago. She is the author of more than twenty-five books for children and young adults on American, Asian, and African history and culture. (*Tibet*, in Children's Press's Enchantment of the World series, was awarded honorable mention by the National Federation of Press Women.) She has also written numerous newspaper, magazine, and encyclopedia articles.

Ann holds a bachelor's and master's degree in piano performance. These days, her performing arts are tai chi chuan and kung fu sword. She grows epiphytes (air plants) in seashells from St. Augustine's beach.

Photo Credits